# HINDU
# AND
# MUHAMMADAN FESTIVALS

# HINDU AND MUHAMMADAN FESTIVALS

COMPILED FROM

WILSON, WILKINS, CROOKE, SELL, HUGHES AND OTHER WRITERS

JOHN MURDOCH

GYAN

*Published by*

Gyan Publishing House
5, Ansari Road
Daryaganj, New Delhi-110002
Phone: 011-47034999, 9811692060
E-mail: books@gyanbooks.com

*Distribution Network*
gyanbooks.com
India, USA, Canada, UK, Australia, France



ISBN : 978-81-212-3477-1 (PB)
First Published, 1904

2nd Impression 2020

*Printed at:* Gyan Press, Delhi.



The book at your disposal is the edition of an old book originally published long back. The Text quality of this book may not be at par as compared to our other books but many readers approached us to reprint this important book so that it could satiate their hunger. We request all the readers of this book to help us to improve its quality by providing the necessary text of those pages which are not properly visible. Your valuable support in this case will be highly appreciated and acknowledged and our future readers will be benefitted immensely.

# HINDU AND MUHAMMADAN FESTIVALS.

COMPILED FROM WILSON, WILKINS, CROOKE, SELL, HUGHES, AND OTHER WRITERS.

BY

JOHN MURDOCH, LL.D.

FIRST EDITION, TWO THOUSAND

THE CHRISTIAN LITERATURE SOCIETY FOR INDIA:
LONDON, MADRAS AND COLOMBO.

1904.

## NOTE.

Except where otherwise stated, the account of Hindu Festivals till the Holi inclusive, is taken from *The Religious Festivals of the Hindus* by Professor H. H. Wilson. It originally appeared in the *Journal of the Royal Asiatic Society*, Vol. IX., pp. 60—110 and was reprinted in 1862 in the edition of his *Works* by Dr. R. Rost.

Much use has been made of a pamphlet on *Hindu Festivals*, published in Calcutta. It originally appeared in the *Calcutta Christian Observer* in 1836. A revised edition by the Rev. Dr. K. S Macdonald, appeared in the *Indian Evangelical Review*. This was reprinted by the Christian Literature Society, Calcutta Branch, price one anna. It deals specially with festivals in Bengal. The following compilation seeks to cover the whole of India, but there are local festivals too numerous to be described.

The account of the Muhammadan Festivals is chiefly abridged from Canon Sell's *Faith of Islam*, with some remarks from *The Dictionary of Islam* by Hughes.

J. M.

# PREFACE.

## To Missionaries and Zenana Workers.

One great difficulty everywhere in India is to secure attention to the Gospel Message. The people have no deep sense of sin, and do not feel the need of the Physician of souls. On the contrary, they are warmly interested in their festivals; among the women especially they are for the time their absorbing thought.

Christian workers should, therefore, have a good acquaintance with the principal festivals, their origin, the legends connected with them, and their mode of celebration. Besides being used as starting points for Christian addresses, it is desirable to have cheap tracts on the principal festivals, which might be offered for sale when they are about to be celebrated. Zenana workers might thus circulate a large number of copies.

The festivals are arranged chronologically; but the dates vary more or less. Almanacks will show the precise times for each year.

# CONTENTS.

## I. HINDU FESTIVALS.

## II. MUHAMMADAN FESTIVALS.

# INDEX.

# I. HINDU FESTIVALS

## INTRODUCTION.*

AMONG all the nations of the ancient world a considerable portion of the year was devoted to the solemnization of public festivals, at which the people found in the assemblage of multitudes, in the exhibition of games, and in religious pageants and ceremonies, a compensation for the want of those more refined entertainments which are created by the necessities and the luxury of a more advanced stage of civilization. Some of these primitive celebrations have retained their hold upon national tastes and feelings long after their origin and meaning were forgotten, and become interwoven with new conditions of society, with altered manners and institutions, and with a total change of religion. In all the countries of Europe they have left at least traces of their former prevalence in the nomenclature of our calendars, and many of the holidays which are appropriated to the saints of the Christian Church have been borrowed from the public festivals of ancient paganism. In proportion also as nations, or as different classes of the same nation, retain their primitive habits, the observances of olden times enjoy their veneration, and interest their affections. They are, however, fast fading in the Western world, even from the faith of tradition, before the extension of knowledge and refinement, and before the augmented demands for toil which the present artificial modes of life impose, when holidays are denounced as an unprofitable interruption of productive industry, and a festival or a fair is condemned as a wasteful expenditure of time and money. It is only, therefore, in regions remote from the reach of the taskmaster, where exemption from work is occasionally the equal right of all classes of the community, that we may expect to find the red letters of the Calendar significant signs—importing what they designate—public holidays—days on which the artificer and the peasant rest from physical exertion, and spend some passing hours in a kindly communion of idleness with their fellows, in which, if the plough stands still and the anvil is silent, the spirit of social intercourse is kept alive, and man is allowed to feel that he was born for some nobler end than to earn the scanty bread of the pauper by the unrelaxing labour of the slave.

* From Wilson's *Essays on the Religion of the Hindus*, Vol. II., p. 151.

It is in the remote East, and especially in India, that we may expect to find the living representation of ancient observances, and the still existing solemnizations which delighted the nations of antiquity, and we shall not be altogether disappointed; although even here they begin to languish under the influence of a foreign government, under the unsympathizing superiority which looks upon the enjoyments of a different race with disdain, under the prevalence of the doctrine which regards public holidays as deductions from public wealth, and under the principles of a system of religious faith which, although it might be indulgent to popular recreations, cannot withhold its disapprobation of them when their objects and origin are connected with falsehood and superstition. From the operation of these causes, the Hindu festivals have already diminished both in frequency and in attraction; and they may become, in the course of time, as little familiar to the people of India as those of European institution are to the nations of the West. They will then, perhaps, become also objects of curiosity and interest; and in anticipation of that period, and in order to secure an account of them whilst it is still possible to learn what they are, I propose to offer to the Society some notices of the religious Fasti of the Hindus and Calendar of their public festivals.

The different celebrations of the Hindus are specified in their Almanacs, and are described at length in different works, such as the Tithi Tattwa, Tithi Kritya, Vratárka, Kála Nirnaya, the Kalpa Druma of Jaya Sinha, and others, and also in passages of several of the Puránas, particularly in the Bhavishyottara, which, as it usually occurs, treats exclusively of the festivals. The observances are, for the most part, the same in the different provinces of India, but there are some peculiar to peculiar localities; and even those which are universally held, enjoy various degrees of popularity in different places, and are celebrated with various local modifications. The periods also vary within certain limits, according as the lunar month is reckoned to begin from the new moon, or from the full moon; the former mode of computation prevailing in Bengal and in Telingana, whilst in Hindustan and in the Tamil countries of the South the latter is followed.* My opportunities of personal observation have been in a great degree limited to Bengal, and for the rest of India I can speak but imperfectly of any existing practices which may not exactly conform to those enjoined by original works, or of which no account has been published by actual observers. One object of communicating these notices to the Society is, therefore, the supplying of this deficiency. Amongst the Members of the

* [Prinsep's Useful Tables, ed. E. Thomas, p. 154 f.]

Society* are many who, in the course of their public services, must have witnessed the celebration of the Hindu festivals in different and distant places: their better knowledge will enable them to furnish correct information respecting those local peculiarities with which I am unacquainted; and I hope that they may be induced to favour the Society with the results of their experience, and contribute to render the description of the popular festivals of the Hindus as complete and authentic as those who may take an interest in the topic have a right to expect from us.

Upon examining the Fasti of the nations of antiquity, it is obvious that many of their festivals originated either from the same or similar motives. They all bear a religious character, inasmuch as religious worship formed part of the celebration; but that was the spirit of the time. However erroneously directed, the feelings of the multitude in the heathen world associated the powers of heaven, real or imaginary, with all their transactions; but the sources to which I more especially refer, however closely linked with this common sentiment, are in some degree varieties of it: they constitute the species, and are obviously reducible to two principal distinctions, which may be regarded as universal or particular. The universal festivals, which are probably traceable among all nations elevated above barbarism, and which may have been handed down by tradition from the earliest periods in the history of the human race, are manifestly astronomical, and are intended to commemorate the revolutions of the planets, the alternations of the seasons, and the recurrence of cyclical intervals of longer or shorter duration. The particular festivals are those arising out of national forms of religious worship, out of the different mythological creations of priests or poets, or out of imperfect narratives, transmitted orally through succeeding generations, of occurrences anterior to historical record. In as far as these traditions may have related to the great mass of mankind, before it was broken up into detached communities, or as the mythological fictions may typify real personages or events of the same era, or may embody objects likely to be presented to the imaginations of men under similar aspects, we need not be surprised to meet with analogies of deep interest, even in the festivals which are of particular institution. It is, however, in those which relate to the course of time and the phenomena of the planetary sphere that analogies are most likely to occur, and do, in fact, present themselves in the practices of distant and apparently unconnected races.

---

* The Bengal Royal Asiatic Society, in whose Journal the account first appeared, 1840. Vol. IX., pp. 10-110.

The coincidences that may be discovered between the universal or particular festivals of the various nations of antiquity, form a subject that well deserves careful and patient investigation. It would, in all probability, tend to confirm the remarkable results which comparative philology has of late so unanswerably demonstrated, and furnish corroborative testimony of that relationship of races, which, however, dissimilar now, in physical configuration, social condition, and national character, are proved to be of kindred origin by the unequivocal affinities of language. In like manner as the Greek, Latin, Teutonic, Celtic, Slavonic, and Sanskrit tongues have been shown to be allied by principles common to them all, so in all probability it would be found that the festivals and holidays which once animated the cities of Athens and Rome, the forests of Germany and the steppes of Russia, are still continuing to afford seasons of public recreation to the dark complexioned tribes that people the borders of the Indus and the Ganges. The full development of these identifications is, however, a work of time and of research exceeding what I can bestow upon it; and I must be content with contributing only that portion of the materials requisite for its investigation which relates to the Fasti of the Hindus, briefly suggesting, as I proceed, one or two of the most obvious points of apparent similarity.

The subject of the Festivals of the Hindu year was introduced to the Asiatic Society of Bengal by Sir William Jones, who published a paper on it in the third volume of the Researches. What he thought of the inquiry is evident from the manner in which he speaks of the authority whence his information was derived, and which he calls a wonderfully curious tract of the learned and celebrated Raghunandana. It was no doubt this Tithi Tattwa, a standard text-book, as are all the works of the same author, in Bengal. Sir William Jones, however, has taken from this work only the heads of the descriptions, and omits all the particulars into which it enters, with the exception of a few brief notes; and his details are neither sufficiently full nor interesting to inspire others with the sentiments with which he contemplated the subject. Some years ago I collected materials for its fuller elucidation, and published in one of the Calcutta papers brief notices of the festivals as they occurred; but the notices were merely popular, and were necessarily short and unconnected, and they have never been presented in a collective form. The topic is one, therefore, which, if destitute of other recommendation, possesses, even in these latter days, that of some degree of novelty, and may on this account be further acceptable to the Society.

As remarked by Sir William Jones, although most of the Indian fasts and festivals are regulated by the days of the moon, yet the most solemn and remarkable of them have a manifest reference to the supposed motions of the sun. An attempt is usually made to adjust the one to the other; but the principles on which the adjustment of the solar to the lunar year is based, are of a somewhat complicated character, and are not essential to a knowledge of the periods at which the festivals are held, and which, with a few exceptions, are sufficiently determinate. They will be specified as we proceed.

## UTTARÁYANA.

*First of (solar month) Mágha, first lunation dark half or Moon's wane of Pausha or Mágha, 12th-13th of January.*—The Roman poet Ovid, in the opening of his "Fasti,"* inquires of Janus why the new year is considered to begin in January instead of April, in winter instead of spring; as the latter is the true season of the renovation of nature, when flowers bud, birds carol, and animals rejoice.

The same question seems to have suggested itself to the reformers of the Hindu calendar, and accordingly the new year of the luni-solar computation now in use begins with the first of Chaitra, which falls somewhere in the course of March, and in solar reckoning is said to agree with the entrance of the sun into the sign Mesha, or Aries. There was, however, a period at which a different principle was followed,† and one that coincides with the peculiarity that puzzled the poet; the new year then commenced on the first of the solar month Mágha, the date of the Makara-Sankránti, or sun's entrance into the sign Capricornus,‡ identical with the Uttaráyana, or return of that luminary to the regions of the North, or, in fact, to the winter solstice; a very important era to the nations north of the equator, amongst whom no doubt were the primitive Hindus, as bringing back to them the genial warmth of the sun and the resuscitation of vegetable life, and deservedly, therefore, held to be the beginning of a new year.

The Uttaráyana, or winter solstice, although no longer considered as occurring on the first day of the year, and which, even in olden times, as we shall see, was thrown back a fortnight, to the first of the light half of Pausha, retains the veneration attached to it originally as the renovator of animal and vegetable

* [v. 149.]

† According to Bentley, this was 1181 B.C. [Historical View of Hindu Astronomy, p. 30.]

‡ The term Makara denotes an aquatic non-descript animal: the more ancient name of the sign seems to have been Mriga, a deer, "The two Sankrántis, the deer and the crab."—Tithi Tattwa. The same work explains the application of the term, the type of the constellation having the head, not of a goat, but of a deer [See Weber, "Indische Studien," II., 299, 415.]

existence, and is one of the great festivals of the Hindus. It commences, as in our own calendars, with the entrance of the sun into the sign Capricornus; but, although the astronomical period is the same, the actual dates present a considerable deviation. According to our Ephemerides, the sun enters Capricorn on the 21st of December; according to those of the Hindus, on the 1st of their solar month Mágha; and this, in actual practice, is identified with the 12th of January or thereabouts. I have already observed that the adjustments of the Hindu calendar are very difficult matters to deal with, and an explanation of the difference between the 21st of December and the 12th of January is to be found only in astronomical calculations. Thus Colonel Warren observes, the dates of the equinoctial and solstitial points, as far as they are regulated by the solar and lunar moveable zodiac, are fixed, but their relation to the sidereal zodiac depends upon the precessional variation.* For our present purpose, however, it is sufficient to know that the essential elements of the celebration are the Makara Sankránti, or sun's entrance into Capricorn; the Uttaráyana, or commencement of the sun's return to a northern declination; and the actual observance on the 1st of the luni-solar month Mágha falling on the 12th of January; or occasionally a day before or after it.

The observances enjoined on this occasion are partly of a private, partly of a public character. The first consist of offerings to the Pitris, or progenitors, whether general, as of all mankind; or special, as of the family of the worshipper; to the Vástu devas, the Dii Lares, or domestic genii; the guardians of the dwelling, or the site on which it is erected; and to the Viswa devas, or universal gods. The ceremonies addressed to all these are performed within the abode of the householder, and are conducted by the family priest. The principal article of the offering is tila, or sesamum seeds, either separately, or, as is more usual, mixed with molasses, or the saccharine juice of the fruit of the date-tree, and made up into a kind of sweetmeat, called Tilüá. Pishtakas or cakes also are offered, composed of ground rice, mixed with sugar and ghee; whence the festival has the denomination of Tilüá Sankránti and Pishtaka Sankránti, the solar conjunction of the sweetmeat or the cake.

The good things prepared on this occasion are not intended exclusively for those imaginary beings who are unable to eat them. They are presented merely for the purpose of consecration, and that they may be eaten with greater zest by the householder and his family; nor is that all, for a portion of them is

---

* Kála Sankalitá, p. 4, note. [Journal of the American Oriental Soc., VI., 249.] The Hindus were ignorant of the precession of the equinoxes. Their Almanacks represent the heavens as they existed many centuries ago.

sent to friends and relations, as memorials of regard, inclosed in fine linen, silk, or velvet, according to the means of the presenter, and the station of those to whom they are presented.

In many places in Bengal a curious practice is observed, called Báwanna bandhana, particularly by the females of the family. In the evening, one of the women takes a wisp of straw, and from the bundle picks out separate straws, which she ties singly to every article of furniture in the house, exclaiming "Báwanna pauti," implying, may the measure of corn be increased fifty-two fold,—pauti denoting a measure of grain. In the villages similar straws are attached to the Golas, or thatched granaries in which the grain of the preceding harvest has been stored.

Besides these private ceremonies, which expressively typify the feelings of satisfaction with which the re-approach of the sun was hailed by a people to whom the principal phenomena of the heavens were familiar,* there are also public celebrations of the same event, expressing similar sentiments, but deriving a more local and peculiar complexion from the physical circumstances of the country, and the superstitions of its inhabitants.

According to the Kalpa Druma of Jayasinha, upon the authority of the Padma Purána, the whole month of Mágha is especially consecrated to Vishnu, to whom and to the Sun also prayers should be daily addressed, and offerings or arghyas presented. The introduction of Vishnu is a modern interpolation.† The same work prescribes daily bathing before sunrise. The Bhavishyottara‡ also directs daily bathing in Mágha, with mantras or prayers by the three first classes, silently by Súdras and women, and affirms that the practice is enjoined by the Vedas, a rather questionable assertion. The same may be said of the Vaishnava formulæ, given by Raghunandana; according to whom the person performing his ablutions is to invoke various personifications of Vishnu. Thus the Sankalpa, or previous prayer, is, "By this bathing, when the sun is in Makara, be thou, oh Mágha, oh Govinda, oh Achyuta, oh Mádhava, oh God, the giver of the promised reward to me." He is then to bathe, calling to mind Vásudeva, Hari, Krishna, Srídhara, and to say, "Salutation be to thee, oh Sun, lord of the world, giver of light, do thou make perfect this great worship, this bathing in Mágha."§

---

* It was considered inauspicious to die during the Dakshináyana, while the sun was going to the south. Bhíshma, in the Mahábhárata, when wounded, wished to live till the Uttaráyana.

† The ablution is to be preceded by a fast and followed by a feast and gifts to Brahmans. Tithi T.

‡ [c. 107.]

§ Sabdakalpadruma s. v. mágha, p. 3394. The Nirnayasindhu (71, b, 8, Benares edition) reads उषपते instead of महाव्रतम्.

Whatever may be the date of this mixture of tenets, the ablution is no doubt an ancient portion of the rite. Bathing in sacred streams constitutes an indispensable part of most of the ceremonial observances of the Hindus; and where such rivers are not within access, their place is supplied by other pieces of water of less lofty pretensions; a dirty puddle may take the place of the holy Gangá. At the winter solstice, bathing at the confluence of the Ganges with the ocean is particularly meritorious, and accordingly a vast concourse of people is annually assembled at Gangá Ságar, or the mouth of the Hugli branch of the Ganges, at the period of the Makara Sankránti, agreeably to the limitations above assigned to it; that is, its identification with the 1st of Mágha or the 12th of January Wherever such assemblages take place, objects of a secular nature are now, as they have ever been, blended with those of devotion; and the Melá, which originates in purposes of pilgrimage, becomes equally or in a still greater degree a meeting of itinerant merchants, or a fair.*

The number of persons who assemble at Gangá Ságar is variously estimated. Some years ago they were considered to average about one hundred thousand; but I have been informed by high authority that latterly the number has increased to double that amount. They come from all parts of India, the larger proportion, of course, from the contiguous provinces of Bengal and Orissa; but there are many from the Dakhan and from Hindustan, and even from Nepal and the Panjáb. They are of both sexes and of all ages; many come with small pedlery for petty traffic; many from idleness or a propensity to a vagrant life, not uncommon in India; and there is a very large proportion of religious mendicants of all sects. The Saivas usually predominate.

The place at which the Melá is held is, or perhaps it were more safe to say, was, some years ago, a sand bank, on the southern shore of the island of Ságar, immediately to the west of the inlet called Pagoda Creek, from a small pagoda or temple, also on the west of the creek, nearer to the sea than the bank of sand, and separated from the latter by a smaller creek running inland. South from this to the sea-shore, extended a thick jungle, with a pathway leading into the interior, where was a large tank for the supply of the people with fresh water. Tigers lurked in the jungle, and not unfrequently carried off the pilgrims. Along the sea-side, for more than a mile, extended rows of booths, shops, and small temporary temples, with the travelling gods of the religious mendicants, who received the adoration and contributions of the pious. Besides the numerous shops for the supply

* [G. de Tassy, Mémoire sur les particularités de la religion Musulmane dans l'Inde. Paris: 1831, p. 26 ff.]

of provisions and sweetmeats, a brisk traffic was carried on in small wares, especially in betel-nuts, black pepper, and the red powder that is scattered about at the vernal festival of the Hugli. A Pandit in my employ, who had visited the Melá, asserted that an impost was levied by the custom officers of Government, of four ánás per oar on each boat; but no such charge appears to have been authorized, except in the case of the Ságar Island Society, who were permitted to make some such charge in consideration of the clearings and tanks made by them. The mendicants, however, petitioned against this privilege, and it was withdrawn from the Society. The petition was not disinterested, as the Sannyásis claimed a right to levy the charge on their own account; a practice that seems to have grown up from long use, and to have been silently acquiesced in by the pilgrims. The total amount was inconsiderable, having been farmed by a native contractor from the Society, whilst in their possession, for 1,200 rupees in the first year, and 2,000 in the second.

The Melá lasts several days, but three days are the limit of the religious festival. The first ceremony is the propitiation of the ocean, by casting into it various offerings, with short ejaculatory prayers; the oblations are commonly cocoa-nuts, fruits, or flowers; the most appropriate gift is that of the five gems, Pancha ratna, consisting of a pearl or diamond, an emerald, a topaz, and a piece of coral, along with a cocoa-nut, an areca-nut, and the thread worn by Brahmans. These are wrapped up in a cloth, and cast into the branch of the river which communicates with the sea, at a place called Dholá Samudra, and also at the confluence. The jewels are, in general, of the smaller size, not worth more than a rupee or two. There was a time when the offerings were of a less innocent description, and children were cast into the sea. This horrible and unnatural practice was wholly unsanctioned by anything in the Hindu ritual; and its suppression, by the Government of Bengal, had the cordial concurrence of the Brahmans. The act was not, like the oblation of fruits or jewels, intended to obtain the favour of the deified ocean, but in satisfaction of a vow; as where a woman had been childless, she made a vow to offer her first-born at Gangá Ságar, or some other holy place, in the confidence that such an offering would secure for her additional progeny. The belief is not without a parallel in the history of antiquity, sacred or profane, but it was the spontaneous growth of ignorance and superstition, not only unprompted, but condemned by the Hindu religion, and was confined to the lowest orders of the people. It will easily be credited, that the occurrence was rare, and that no attempt has ever been made to infringe the prohibition.

On the first day, bathing in the sea is to be performed; it takes place early in the morning, and is repeated by some at

2

noon; some also have their heads shaved after bathing; and many of those whose parents are recently deceased celebrate their Sráddha, or obsequial ceremonies, on the sea-shore. After ablution, the pilgrims repair to the temple, which is dedicated to a Muni, or divine sage, an incarnation of Vishnu, named Kapila. Vishnu became incarnate in his person for the destruction of the sixty thousand wicked sons of King Sagara. He is said to have stationed himself at this place, which was then upon the brink of a vast chasm leading to the infernal regions. When the sons of the king, who were in search of a horse intended for the solemn sacrifice of the Aswamedha, arrived here, they found the Muni absorbed apparently in meditation, while the steed was grazing near him. Accusing him of having stolen it, they approached to kill him, when fire flashed from his eyes, and instantly reduced the whole troop to ashes. In order to expiate their crime, purify their remains, and secure paradise for their spirits, Bhagíratha, the great-grandson of Sagara, brought down by the force of his austerities the Ganges from heaven; and led her from the Himálaya, where she had alighted, to this spot. The sons of Sagara were sanctified, and the waters of the river, flowing into the chasm, formed the ocean. The Ganges is called Bhágírathí, from King Bhagíratha; and the sea is termed Ságara, after his great-grandsire. The legend is told, in its most ancient and authentic shape, in the Rámáyana.*

The temple of Kapila is under the alternate charge of a Bairágí and Sannyási, mendicants of the Vaishnava and Saiva sects; the latter presides at the Melá held at this place in the month Kártik, the former at the Melá of Mágha. They exact a fee of four ánás from each person who comes to the temple. The aggregate collection of Mágha was divided amongst five different establishments of mendicants of the Rámánandí order, in the vicinity of Calcutta. In front of the temple was a Bur tree, beneath which were images of Ráma and Hanumán, and an image of Kapila, of the size nearly of life, was within the temple. The pilgrims commonly write their names on the walls of the temple, with a short prayer to Kapila; or suspend a piece of earth or brick to a bough of the tree, with some solicitation, as for health, or affluence, or offspring; and promise, if their prayers are granted, to make a gift to some divinity.

Behind the temple was a small excavation termed Sitá kund, filled with fresh water, of which the pilgrim was allowed to sip a small quantity, on paying a fee to the mahant or head manager of the temple. This reservoir was probably filled from the tank, and kept full by the contrivances of the mendicants, who

* [1, 42—45.]

persuaded the people that it was a perpetual miracle, being constantly full for the use of the temple.

On the second and third days of the assemblage, bathing in the sea, adoration of Gangá, and the worship of Kapila, continue as on the first; after which the meeting breaks up. During the whole time the pilgrims, for the most part, sleep on the sand; for it is considered unbecoming to sleep on board their boats.

This is the great public celebration of the recurrence of the winter solstice in Upper India.

## PONGAL.

(*A Southern Festival, January.*)

In South India this festival is a still more popular commemoration of the Winter Solstice than in North India. The following account is from Dubois, the highest authority on the subject.

Of all festivals, the most famous is that which is called *Pongal* (boiling), celebrated at the end of the winter solstice. It lasts three days; during which time the Hindus employ themselves in mutual visits and compliments, something in the same manner as Europeans do on the first day of the year.

The feast of the Pongal is a season of rejoicing for two special reasons. The first is that the month of *Magha* or December, every day in which is unlucky, is about to expire; and the other, that it is to be succeeded by a month, each day of which is fortunate.

The first day of this festival is called Bhogi Pongal or the *Pongal of Rejoicing* or rather the Pongal in honour of Indra, the lord of the season. It is kept by inviting the near relations to an entertainment which passes off with hilarity and mirth.

The second day is called *Súrya Pongal* or *Pongal of the Sun*, and is set apart to the honour of that luminary. Married women after purifying themselves by bathing, which they perform by plunging into the water without taking off their clothes, and coming out all dripping wet, set about boiling rice in the open air, and not under any cover. They use milk in the operation, and when it begins to simmer, they make a loud cry, all at once repeating the words, 'Pongal, O Pongal.' The vessel is then lifted off the fire and set before the idol of Vighnaswara, (Ganesa), which is placed close by. Part of the mass of rice is offered to the image; and after standing there for some time it is given to the cow; and the remainder of the rice is then distributed among the people.

This is the great day of visiting among the Hindus. The salutation begins by the question, 'Has the milk boiled?' to which the answer is 'It has boiled.' From this the festival takes its name of Pongal; which is derived from the verb *Ponghédi* in Telugu, and *Pongu* in Tamil, both of which signify 'to boil.'

The third day, not less solemn than the preceding, is consecrated with ceremonies still more absurd, and is called the *Pongal of Cows*.

In a great vessel filled with water, they put some saffron, the seeds of the cotton tree and leaves of the margosa. After being well mixed, they go round all the cows and oxen belonging to the house, several times sprinkling them with the water as they turn to the four cardinal points. The Sáshtángam, or prostration of the eight members is made before them four times. Men only perform this ceremony, the women staying away.

The cows are then all dressed out, their horns being painted with various colours, and garlands of flowers and foliage being put round their necks and over their backs. They likewise add strings of cocoa-nuts and other fruits, which are soon stricken off by the brisk motion of the animal which these trappings occasion, and are picked up by children and others, who follow the cattle on purpose, and greedily eat what they gather as something sacred. They are then driven, in herd, through the villages, and made to scamper about from side to side by the jarring noise of many sounding instruments. The remainder of the day, they are allowed to feed at large without a keeper; and whatever trespasses they commit are suffered to pass without notice or restraint.*

There can be no doubt that the observance of the Uttaráyana is a practice of high antiquity; and there can be equally little doubt that it was of like universality amongst, at least, the Indo-Teutonic races. The analogies are so obvious, that they must instantly occur to every one's mind; and the offerings and distribution of food and sweetmeats and presents, the sports and the rejoicing, and the interchange of mutual good wishes, which characterize the Uttaráyana amongst the Hindus, are even yet, though to a less extent than heretofore, retained by Christian nations at the same season; beginning with the plum-puddings and mince-pies of Christmas, passing through the new year's gifts and happy new years, the strenæ of the Romans, quæ omnia simul strenas appellarunt; and terminating with Twelfth-night. Whatever modifications these types of rejoicing may have undergone, and however changed in their present purport, by their connexion with our religious faith, they are evidently of the same general character as the observances of the Hindus; and designate

---

* *Manners and Customs of the People of India.* Abridged, pp. 284—286.

the commencement of a period, in which the northern hemisphere is again to be gladdened by the proximity of the fountain of light and heat.

The Romans connected the beginning of the year with the sun's entrance into Capricorn, and then celebrated the renovation of nature. Their mode of celebrating it seems to have had many things in common with the usages of the Hindus, particularly in the interchange of sweetmeats; only substituting for the rice, cakes, and molasses of the Hindus, figs, dates, and honey. These articles they sent, at this season, to their friends and relations: they were intended, according to Janus, to be ominous of an agreeable year to follow.

They also interchanged læta verba, good wishes and congratulations. According to Festus, the practice is referred by Symmachus to an early period of Roman history, the reign of Tacitus; but it was no doubt much older. How far it prevailed among the Greeks does not fully appear.

The Christmas and new year's festivities, which have left traces amongst the Teutonic nations, were transferred to them from their German forefathers, in the time of Paganism. Thus Bede observes of the Anglo-Saxons, "they began their year on the eighth of the calends of January, which is now our Christmas-day." So the yule clog, log or block, which was burnt on the eve of Christmas-day, is considered to have been used as an emblem of the return of the sun, and the lengthening of the days; for, according to Bede, both December and January were denominated Giuli or Yule, upon account of the sun's returning and augmenting the duration of the days.

## Mukkoti Ekadasi or Vaikunta Ekadasi.

(*A Southern Vaishnava Festival.*)

In the Madras Presidency this is a recognised holiday for all Hindus. Every religious Hindu should fast twice in every lunar month—that is the 11th day (*ekádasi*) in each fortnight. These fasts are usually kept in honour of Vishnu, but are not very strictly observed, as fruit and milk are allowed. Hindus generally do not attribute more sanctity to one *ekádasi* than another, but the Vaishnavas consider the Mukkoti or Vaikunta Ekádasi as the holiest of all the Ekádasis. This is because it is said that Nammalwar, one of their Saints, ascended to Vaikuntham, Vishnu's heaven on this day. With the usual exaggeration of Hindus, it is said that the 33 crores of gods came down to witness it. *Mukkoti*, three crores, is a shortened form of *Muppatti Mukkoti* three tens, three crores.*

---

* See *Hindus Feasts, Fasts and Ceremonies* by Pandit Natesa Sastri.

## MANSASHTAKA.

*Eighth lunar day of the dark half of the lunar month Mágha, about the 20th of January.**—The denomination of this day defines its occurrence, *ashtaka* meaning eighth ; it also indicates its purport, *mánsa* signifying flesh. Accordingly, on this day, the *Sráddha*, or obsequial offerings of flesh, should be made to the pitris or manes. According to the Pauránik authorities,† there are three days of this nature, in the months severally of Agraháyana, Mágha, and Phálguna, which is also the specification of Gobhila, as quoted by Raghunandana. But according to the Mitákshará, there are four such ashtakás in the course of the year; there being one on the eighth of the moon's wane of each of the two months of the two seasons of Hemanta and sisira, or the four winter months, when sráddhas are positively enjoined (nitya). The former authorities direct that different offerings shall be made on the three days, or severally, cakes, flesh, and vegetables, as will be noticed. The institution appears to have been part of the ancient ritual, and to have fallen into comparative neglect. The Brahmans of Upper India, who maintain a perpetual fire, and are thence called Agnihotras, are said to observe the Mánsáshtaka ; so do the orthodox Saivas and Sáktas, and the disciples of Raghunandana in Bengal ; but it is usual to substitute cakes of boiled rice flour,‡ mixed with milk and sugar for the meat which was anciently presented, not only at the Ashtaká sráddhas, but, as Manu enjoins, at the periodical sráddhas in general. "Let the Brahman who maintains a household fire, who has performed the funeral ceremonies of his own family, repeat the subsequent general sráddha at the conjunction of the moon every month. The wise have called the monthly sráddhas the subsequent, or periodical sráddha, and that is to be offered diligently with excellent flesh." (B. III., 122, 123.) The time is specified in the Mitákshará, upon the authority of an ancient lawgiver, Aswaláyana.§ The flesh should be that of a goat or a deer, King Ikshwáku having commanded a large deer to be brought to him for the sráddha at the Ahtaká.

## RATANTI CHATURDASI.

*Fourteenth lunar day of the dark half of Mágha (26th January).*—In Sir William Jones's description of this festival, he

---

* The specification of the date is to be understood as applicable to Bengal, and even there it is subject to occasional variation.

† The Vishnu Purána [III., 14] specifies three altogether Aghan, Mágha, and Phálguna. Raghunandana quotes the Brahma P. for the same. [In the Sráddhaviveka (12, r, 1. 2) Pausha takes the place of Aghan.]

‡ Boiled in a pot, sthálipáka, as Gobhila says.

§ [Grihya S. II., 4. cf. Páraskara's Gr. S. III., 2.]

|| [Vishnu Pur. IV., 2.]

merely explains it by the sentence, "The waters speak," the word "ratanti," meaning "they speak;" being the first part of an ancient text importing, "The waters say, We purify the sinner who bathes in the month of Mágha, when the sun is scarcely risen, although he be a chándála, or the killer of a Brahman."* Accordingly the essential rite on this day is bathing in some sacred stream or piece of water; which should be performed before dawn, whilst the stars are yet visible. As in many parts of India the temperature of the atmosphere is at this season almost cold, bathing at such an hour in the open air may easily be conceived to be no trifling penance. Offerings should also be presented on this occasion to Yama, the judge of the lower regions; for he who worships Yama at this period, it is said, shall not see death.† Besides the usual libations of water to deceased progenitors, a sráddha should be celebrated, and Brahmans and the family should be fed with rice mixed with pulse, accompanied by a particular Mantra.‡

These appear to be the ancient directions for a religious rite on the 14th of the dark half of the Mágha; but later days have changed both its time and object. According to the present practice, in Bengal at least, ablution is performed, not before sunrise, but after sunset; and instead of Yama one of the terrific forms of Deví is worshipped, Mundamáliní, she with the chaplet of skulls, or Syámá, the black goddess; particularly when any cause has prevented the adoration of the latter in the month of Kártik. The authority for this modification of the ceremony is that of the Tantras; and, except by the Sáktas, is not held in much estimation. The day is little observed anywhere.

## VARADA CHATURTHI.

*Fourth lunar day of the light half of Maghá (30th January —1st February).*—According to some of the authorities§ followed in Hindustan, Siva is to be worshipped on this day in the evening, with offerings of jasmine flowers, whence it is also called Kunda Chaturthí; but the more usual designation Varadá Chaturthí implies a goddess, the giver of boons, who in some of the Puránas is identified with Gaurí, or more especially with Umá, the bride of Siva. She is on this day to be worshipped with offerings of flowers, of incense, or of lights, with platters of sugar and ginger, or milk, or salt, with scarlet or saffron-tinted strings and golden bracelets. She is to be worshipped

* Harivansa, as cited by Raghunandana.
† [Sabdakalpadruma s. v. Mágha, p. 3395, a.]
‡ As in the Nirnayámrita, from the Brahma Purána.
§ Hemádri, Nirnayámrita, Padma Purána.

by both sexes, but especially by women; and women themselves, not being widows, are also to be treated with peculiar homage. In the Deví Purána it is enjoined, that various kinds of grain, and condiments, and confections, and plates made of baked clay, should be given on this day by maidens to the goddess. The due observance of the rite is said to secure a flourishing progeny. The worship of Gaurí, at this season, seems to be popular in the South of India, as the Calendar specifies the 2nd, 3rd, and 4th of Mágha to be equally consecrated to her. In Bengal little regard is paid to this celebration, although worship is sometimes offered to Umá, on behalf of unmarried females, in reference to the means adopted by Gaurí or Umá, whilst yet a maiden, to propitiate Siva, and obtain him for her husband.* This last circumstance renders it not unlikely, that the epithet Varadá ought to be differently interpreted, and that it means the giver of a husband, a bridegroom being one sense of Vara, and the part which is assigned in it to unmarried girls, the presents to be made by and to them—the offerings to be made for them—and the reward of the rite—a family of children, leave little doubt of the correctness of the interpretation.

## Sri Panchami or Saraswati Puja.

*Fifth lunar day of the light half of the month Mágha* (*2nd February*).—The designation Srí indicates the bride of Vishnu, the goddess of prosperity and abundance; and the text quoted from the Samvatsara Pradípa, in the Tithi Tattwa, confirms the identification by stating, that upon this day, Lakshmí, the goddess of fortune, (who is also the bride of Vishnu), is to be worshipped with flowers, perfumes, food, and water: probably the day was originally dedicated to her. The same text, however, proceeds to direct, that pens, and ink, and books, should be reverenced upon this day; and that a festival should be observed in honour of Saraswatí, the goddess of learning—hence it is inferred, that by Srí, in the first part of the rubric, Saraswatí also is intended, especially as Srí had various significations, one of which may be Saraswatí.

Saraswatí, by the standard mythological authorities, is the wife of Brahmá, and the goddess presiding over letters and arts. The Vaishnavas of Bengal have a popular legend, that she was the wife of Vishnu, as were also Lakshmí and Gangá. The ladies disagreed, Saraswatí, like the other prototype of learned ladies, Minerva, being something of a termagant, and Vishnu, finding

* See Sir Wm. Jones's Ode to Bhavání; also translation of Kumára Sambhava, by Dr. Mill, Journal As. S. B., Vol. II., p. 329.

that one wife was as much as even a god could manage, transferred Saraswatí to Brahmá, and Gangá to Siva, and contented himself with Lakshmí alone. It is worthy of remark, that Saraswatí is represented as of a white colour, without any superfluity of limbs, and not unfrequently of a graceful figure wearing a slender crescent on her brow, and sitting on a lotus.

On the morning of the fifth lunar day of Mágha, the whole of the pens and inkstands, and the books, if not too numerous and bulky, are collected—the pens, or reeds, cleaned, the inkstands scoured, and the books, wrapped up in new cloth, are arranged upon a platform or a sheet, and are strewn over with flowers and blades of young barley; no flowers except white are to be offered. Sometimes these are the sole objects of adoration; but an image of Saraswatí stands, in general, immediately behind them; or, in place of the image, a water-jar; a not uncommon, although a curious substitute for a god or a goddess, amongst the Hindus.

After performing the necessary rites of ablution, Saraswatí is to be meditated upon, and invited to the place of worship, with some such mental prayer as the following: "May the glorious goddess of speech, she who is of a white complexion and graceful figure, wearing a digit of the moon upon her brow, and carrying an inkstand and a pen in her lotus-like hands,—may she, sitting on her lotus throne, be present for our protection,* and for the attainment of honours and wealth." Water is then to be offered for the washing of her feet; food for her refreshment; flowers, or more costly articles, as pearls and jewels, for her decoration; and three salutations are to be made to her with the mantra, "Reverence to Saraswatí, reverence to Bhadrakálí, reverence to the Vedas, to the Vedángas, to the Vedánta, and to all seats of learning."† Of other mantras addressed to her, the following are given in the Matsya Purána:‡ "As Brahmá, the great father of all, never, oh Saraswatí! lives without thee, so do thou ever be my benefactress." Or, "As the Vedas and all inspired writings, as all the sciences and the arts, are never, oh goddess! independent of thee; so, by thy favour, may my wishes be fulfilled." "In the forms of thy eight impersonations, Lakshmí, Medhá, Dhará, Pushtí, Gaurí, Tushti, Prabhá, and Dhriti, do thou, oh Saraswatí! be ever my protectress."

At the end of the ceremony, all the members of the family assemble and make their prostrations—the books, the pens, and

---

* Sáradá Tilaka [6, quoted in the Sabdakalpadruma s. v. Sarasvatí, p. 5975, *b*, (see also p. 1824, *b* and 3395, *b*).
Sir W. Jones translates this prayer somewhat differently.

† Brahma Purána.

‡ [c. 65. Sabdakalpadruma, l. l. (comp. p. 3396, *a*).
See also the Brahmavaivarttapurána, Prakritikhanda, c. 4.]

ink, having an entire holiday; and should any emergency require a written communication on the day dedicated to the divinity of scholarship, it is done with chalk or charcoal upon a black or white board.

After the morning ceremony, the boys and young men repair to the country for amusement and sport, and some of these games are of a very European character, as bat and ball, and a kind of prisoner's base. School-boys also used to consider them selves privileged, on this day, to rob the fields and gardens of the villages, but this privilege was stoutly opposed, and was all but extinct some years ago. In the evening there are entertainments according to the means of the parties.

The regular celebration of this festival here terminates, but of late years a supplementary observance forms a plea for a second day's holiday in Bengal. The Bengalis have a great passion for throwing the temporary images of their female divinities into the Ganges. It is a rite especially appropriate to Durga, at the end of the Durgá Pújá; but it has been extended to other goddesses, and amongst them to Saraswatí, at this season. Accordingly, on the sixth lunar day, the image, which is commonly of plastic clay painted, is conveyed in procession to the river side, stripped of its ornaments, and tossed rather unceremoniously into the stream.

There are some remarkable varieties regarding the seasons of this festival, in different parts of India, whether it be considered as dedicated to Saraswatí or to Lakshmí. The Srí panchamí, when applied to the former, is observed in Hindustan in Aswin (August-September), and when to the latter, in Márgasirsha (October-November), as we shall have future occasion to notice, or the present, the fifth of Mágha, is held to be the proper Srí panchamí, and dedicated, not to Saraswatí, but to Lakshmí. There is, however, both in Upper India and in the Dekhan, a festival on the fifth of the light half of Mágha, which is no doubt the original and ancient celebration,—the Vasanta Panchamí, or the vernal feast of the fifth lunar day of Mágha, marking the commencement of the season of Spring, and corresponding, curiously enough, with the specific date fixed for the beginning of Spring in the Roman calendar, the fifth of the ides of February.

After the Vasanta Panchamí, Káma the god of love, and his bride Ratí, pleasure, are to be worshipped with offerings of fruits and flowers.* In general observance, however, Vishnu and Lakshmí now take their places, as there are no temples to Kámadeva;

* Ratí is personified as a young and beautiful female, richly attired and decorated, dancing and playing on the Víná; and Káma is represented as a youth with eight arms, attended by four nymphs,—Pleasure, Affection, Passion, and Power,—bearing the shell, the lotus, a bow and five arrows, and a banner with the Makara,—a figure composed of a goat and a fish, or, as before mentioned, the sign Capricorn.

nor indeed are the celebrations, which probably once occurred at this season, very particularly observed. The day is retained in the calendars, and constitutes a nominal fixed point, from which festivals, which become conspicuous enough a few weeks afterwards, are still said to commence.

## Sitala Shashthi.

*Sixth lunar day of the light half of Mágha (3rd of February).*—This ceremony is of a strictly private character, and is limited to married women who have children. The object is, in the present day, especially to protect them from the small-pox. The observance, however, seems to have had originally no such specific application, but to have been intended to secure, generally, the healthiness of infants*, by the propitiation of a goddess termed, apparently at the original institution of this rite, Shashthí, but now more commonly Sítalá. According to the legend, the ceremony was instituted by King Priyavrata, in gratitude to Shashthí for restoring his dead son, Suvrata, to life.† It should be celebrated on the sixth day of the light fortnight in every month, but this frequent repetition of it has fallen into disuse. Shashthí is said to be so named because she is a sixth part of the goddess Prakriti, but she evidently derives her name from the day of the fortnight of which she is a personification. She is the daughter of Brahmá, and wife of Kártikeya, the general of the hosts of heaven, and is to be meditated upon as a female dressed in red garments, riding on a peacock and holding a cock. Sítalá, in its ordinary sense, means cold, and is here used as an epithet, in reference, perhaps, to the occasional coolness of the day at this time of the year, as distinguished from the sixth lunar days in other months. The word seems also to have suggested the principal observance on this occasion. Cooking on this day is interdicted, victuals must be dressed on the day preceding, and on this eaten cold. Images of Shashthí are rarely made, but sometimes a small doll represents the goddess, or she is typified by the stone on which condiments are ground. This is covered with a yellow cloth and placed upon a platform; or in villages, at the foot of the Indian fig-tree. Fruits and flowers are offered to it, with this prayer, "Oh, Shashthí! as thou art cold, do thou preserve my children in health."

The worship of Sítala, as identical with Shashthí, seems to be retained only in Bengal. In Hindustan, upon this day, the sun is worshipped with fasting and prayers, and with offerings of Akand or Mandára leaves, whence it is called the Mandara

---

* [See A. K. Forbes, Rás Málá. London: 1856, II, 326 ff.]
† From the Brahma Vaivartta Purána.—Prakriti Khanda, s. 40.

Shashthí. There is, however, a Sitalá Pújá on the eighth of the dark half of Chaitra (or Phálguna), in which case the two minor goddesses are of course distinct.

### BHASKARA SAPTAMI.

*Twenty-second of Mágha, seventh day of the light fortnight (4th of February).*—This day is in an especial degree sacred to the sun. Abstinence is to be practised on the day preceding; and in the morning before sunrise, or at the first appearance of dawn, bathing is to be performed until sunrise; a rigid fast is to be observed throughout the day, worship is to be offered to the sun, presents are to be made to the Brahmans, and in the evening the worshipper is to hold a family feast; one of the observances of the day is abstinence from study, neither teacher nor scholar being allowed to open a book.

At the time of bathing, certain prayers are to be mentally recited, during which the bather places upon his head a platter holding seven leaves of the arka plant (calotropis gigantea), or satávarí (asparagus racemosus), or the jujube, or a little oil and a lighted wick, and stirs the water around him, according to some, with a piece of sugar-cane; after his prayers, he removes the articles from his head, and sets the lamp afloat on the water. He then makes the usual libations to the Manes, and having gone home, presents food. and money, and clothes, according to his means, to the Brahmans. One of the formulæ of meditation given is, "Glory to thee, who art a form of Rudra, to the lord of Rasas, to Varuna, oh Hárivása, be salutation to thee."

The Kásí Khanda, as quoted in the Kalpa Druma, gives a different prayer: "Of whatever sin committed by me during seven lives, may this Mákarí Saptamí remove both the sorrow and the shame,* and whatever sin has been committed by me in this life, through the influence of time, whether in mind, spirit, or body, wittingly or unwittingly, may every such sin, involving the fruit of seven diseases, be effaced by this bathing, oh thou who art identical with the sun, do thou efface it, oh Mákarí Saptamí!" The repetition of this prayer purifies a person from all sin, and the whole rite is considered as securing him from sickness and premature decay.

As appears from these latter mantras, the day is also termed Mákarí Saptamí, the seventh lunar day of the sun in Capricornus. It may be doubted if the term Mákarí is rightly understood, even by the original authorities. Raghunandana considers it to designate the whole month of Mágha, which, regarded as a solar month, should commence with the sun's entrance into the sign.

* [Sabdak. d., p. 3391, *a*, and Nirnayasindhu, c. II, p. 73 *b*.]

There may, however, be something more in it, and it may originally have been identical with the Uttaráyana, when the sun is equally an especial object of adoration, and either a change of computation depending on astronomical periods, or the purpose of multiplying festivals, has detached it from its primitive position.

In Upper India, the day is also called Achalá Saptamí, the fixed or immovable seventh, because it is said it is always to be held sacred. In the South it is better known as the Ratha Saptamí, or Seventh of the Chariot; for it is also the first day of Manwantara, or period of the reign of a Manu, being that of Vivaswat, when the sun comes abroad in a new carriage. Agreeably to the directions given in the Kalpa Taru, for the proper observance of this rite, the sun should be worshipped in his own temple—a temple it would now be difficult to discover in any part of India—with prayers and offerings upon the sixth; during which abstinence is to be practised, and at night the worshipper is to sleep on the ground. He is to bathe and fast on the seventh, as before described, but he is also to construct a car of gold, or silver, or wood, with horses and driver; and after the mid-day ablutions, to decorate it, and with prayers from the Vedas invite the sun to take his place in it. Worship is then to be addressed to the sun, and the worshipper is to prefer whatever desire he may have formed, which the sun will assuredly grant him. The night is to be spent with music, singing, and rejoicing, and in the morning ablution is to be repeated; presents are to be made to the Brahmans, and the car with all its appurtenances is to be presented to the Guru or spiritual preceptor. This is probably an ancient rite, coeval with the development of the institutions of the Vedas.

Various other appellations are specified as belonging to this same lunar day, as the Jayantí Saptamí, the victorious seventh; the Mahá Saptamí, the great seventh, and others; but the characteristic observance is the same, and whatever the designation, the worship of the sun is the prominent ceremony of the seventh of the light half of Mágha.

The same may be said, however, of the seventh lunar day throughout the year, chiefly of one-seventh in each fortnight, that of the moon's increase; but also of the seventh day of the wane. Besides which, there are particular sevenths to which the concurrence of other circumstances, such as its falling on a Sunday*, or when the moon enters certain mansions, as Rohiní, gives extraordinary sanctity, and renders the worship of the sun more than usually efficacious. The specification of the days of the week by the names of the seven planets is, as it is well

* [From the Bhavishyapuráńa, quoted in the Sabdakalpadruma, p. 5891, a.]

known, familiar to the Hindus. The origin of this arrangement is not very precisely ascertained, as it was unknown to the Greeks and not adopted by the Romans until a late period. It is commonly ascribed to the Egyptians and Babylonians, but upon no very sufficient authority, and Hindus appear to have, at least, as good a title as any other people to the invention.

Aditya-vára, Ravi-várá, or Rabi-bár in the barbarized vernacular, Dies Solis, or Sunday, is one of every seven. This is somewhat different from the seventh Tithi or lunar day, but a sort of sanctity is, or at least was, attached even to Sunday, and fasting on it was considered obligatory or meritorious.* But the religious Fasti of the Hindus confine their instructions to the Tithi, and declare, that whoever worships the sun, on the seventh day of the moon's increase, with fasting, and offerings of white oblations, as white flowers and the like, and whoever fasts on the seventh of the moon's wane, and offers to the sun red flowers and articles of a red colour, is purified from all iniquity and goes after death to the solar sphere.† The worship of the sun, on the seventh of the dark fortnight, seems to have gone out of use, but that on the seventh of the light fortnight is strongly recommended in various authorities, beginning with this seventh of Mágha and continuing throughout the year. In connexion with this observance, different modes of abstinence are enjoined for each succeeding lunar day, such as taking, during the day, small quantities only of milk, or ghee, or water, or acrid leaves; or fasting wholly from sunset on the sixth till after morning ablutions on the eighth; thence this day is also termed Vidhána Saptamí—the seventh of observance—as being the first of the series. On all these occasions Arghyas, or offerings, are presented to the Sun; but the arghya, more peculiarly appropriated to him, consists of eight articles. These slightly vary in different specifications, but they are usually water, milk, curds, ghee, sesamum and mustard seeds, grains of rice, and the blossom of the kusa grass. Perfumes and flowers, especially of a white or a red colour, are also most fit to be presented to the sun, according to some authorities. Gifts of fuel, and the lighting of a large fire on the morning of the seventh lunar day of Mágha, are also meritorious acts. The following are two other prayers‡ usual on these occasions, in which it will be noticed that the number "Seven" makes a conspicuous figure.

Upon presenting the Argha, the day itself personified as a goddess is thus addressed; "Mother of all creatures, Saptamí! who art one with the lord of the seven coursers and the seven

---

* The jackal declines touching the sinewy meshes of the noose, because it is Sunday.—Hitopadesa [I, p. 21, l. 21, ed. Lassen et Schlegel.

† Commentary on Tithi Tattwa.

‡ From the Narasinha Purána.

mystic words, glory to thee in the sphere of the sun;" and on prostration before the sun or his image, the worshipper utters, "Glory to thee, who delightest in the chariot drawn by seven worlds; glory to thee on the seventh lunar day—the infinite, the creator!"* It is impossible to avoid inferring, from the general character of the prayers and observances, and the sanctity evidently attached to a recurring seventh day, some connexion with the sabbath, or seventh, of the Hebrew Heptameron.

## Bhishmashtami.

*Twenty-third of Mágha, eighth lunar day of the light half (7th February).*—This is a festival which, at first sight, appears to be of special and traditional origin, but which has, probably, its source in the primitive institutes of the Hindus, of which the worship of the Pitris, the patriarchs or progenitors, the Dii Manes, constituted an important element. According to the Tithi Tattwa, this day is dedicated to Bhíshma, the son of Gangá, and great uncle of the Pándava and Kaurava princes; who was killed in the course of the great war, and dying childless left no descendant in the direct line, on whom it was incumbent to offer him obsequial honours. In order to supply this defect, persons in general are enjoined to make libations of water on this day to his spirit, and to offer him sesamum seeds and boiled rice. The act expiates the sins of a whole year: one of its peculiarities is, that it is to be observed by persons of all the four original castes, according to a text of Dhavala, an ancient lawgiver, quoted by Raghunandana, "Oh twice-born! persons of all the Varnas should on the eighth lunar day offer water, sesamum seeds, and rice, to Bhíshma. If a Brahman, or man of any other caste, omit to make such offerings the merit of his good deeds during the preceding year is annulled According to a different reading of the text, however, it should be rendered: "Let all the twice-born castes make the oblations."† This excludes Súdras, but extends the duty to the Kshatriyas and Vaisyas as well as Brahmans. The intention of the rite, as now understood, is expressed in the formulæ uttered at the time of presenting the offerings: "I present this water to the childless hero Bhíshma, of the race of Vyághrapada, the chief of the house of Sankriti. May Bhíshma the son of Santanu, the speaker of truth and subjugator of his passions, obtain by this water the oblations due by sons and grandsons."‡ The simple nature of the

* Sabdakalpadruma s. v. Saptamí p. 5896, *b* (comp. p. 3396, *b*) and, with some various readings, Nirnayasindhu, l. 1.

† Sabdak.d., p. 2980 f. Hemádri ap. Nirnayasindhu, c. II, 74, *a*.]

‡ Sabdak.d., p. 2981, *a*. Nirnayasindhu, c. II, p. 74, *a*. Pránatoshaní f. 172, *b*, 2.]

offerings which are sufficient on such occasions, water and sesamum seeds, justifies the remark made by Ovid on the Feralia, that the Manes are easily satisfied,—Parva petunt manes.

The observance of this ceremony is almost obsolete in Bengal, and in the principal authorities of Hindustan it is not noticed. The Bhavishyottara Purána* has a Bhíshma panchakam, —a solemn rite which begins on the 11th of Kártik (light half), and continues to the 13th, which has something of the character of the Feralia, being a period of mortification and fasting, and expiatory of sin, which is worshipped in an effigy made for the occasion, placed upon a measure of sesamum, and invoked by the appellations of Dharmarájá or Yama, the judge of the dead. The ceremony is said to have been ordained by Bhíshma, when mortally wounded, and is to be practised by all castes, and even by women. The rite is not found, however, in any of the calendars, and it is probably an expiring relique of the once general and public worship of the Manes.

## BHAIMYEKADASI.

*Eleventh lunar day of the light half of Mágha (10th February).* —This is also a festival of traditional origin, said to have been first observed by Bhíma, one of the Pandu princes, in honour of Vishnu, according to the instructions of Vásudeva. Every eleventh lunar day, it may be observed, is held in extravagant veneration by the Hindus, but more particularly by the Vaishnavas. Fasting on the eleventh is declared to be equally efficacious with a thousand aswamedhas, and eating during its continuance as heinous a sin as parricide, or the murder of a spiritual teacher. This extravagance demonstrates its sectarian character, and consequently its more modern origin. The notion may have grown, however, out of particular appropriations of the lunar day, when the eleventh was set apart, as in the present case, to the adoration of Vishnu.

According to the ritual, the worshipper on this occasion is to fast on the tenth, and bathe at sunset. He is to bathe at dawn on the eleventh, and having previously constructed a temporary temple in the court-yard of his house, he is to cause burnt-offerings to be made to Purushottama and other forms of Vishnu, by Brahmans acquainted with the Vedas; he himself going through a rather complicated series of prayers and gesticulations. There is no image of Vishnu, and he is invoked by formulæ derived from the Vedas. The worshipper observes a strict fast throughout the day, and keeps a vigil at night with music and singing. On the morning of the twelfth he dismisses the Brahmans with presents,

* [c. 63. See also Padmapurána, Uttarakhanda, c. 132, and Garudapurána, c. 128, as quoted in the Sabdak.d. s. v. Bhíshmapanchakam.]

bathes, and then takes a meal, of which flesh forms no part. The performance of this ceremony expiates the sin incurred by omission of any of the prescribed fasts during the preceding twelvemonth.

Some differences of date and nomenclature occur, in various authorities, regarding this day. The Kalpa Druma calls it Jayá, but enjoins fasting and watching, and the worship of Vishnu; and attributes to it the same expiatory efficacy, calling it the purifier, the destroyer of sin, the bestower of all desires, and the granter of emancipation to mankind.—Pavitrá, pápahantrí cha, kámadá, mokshadá nrinám. The same work, however, has a day named from Bhíma, and refers to the same legend for its origin; but it places it on the following day, as Bhíma dwádasí. The Bhavishyottara Purána* also removes the day to the twelfth, and tells a different story to account for it, describing it as taught by the sage Pulastya to King Bhíma, the father of Damayantí, in reply to his anxious inquiry how sin was to be efficaciously expiated. Like the preceding, its essence is the domestic worship of Vishnu, with the Homa or oblations to fire, and ceremonies and prayers of Vaidika origin. One part of the ceremony consists in the administration of a sort of shower-bath to the institutor of the rite, as towards evening water is dropped upon his head from a perforated vessel, whilst he sits meditating upon Vishnu. The evening is to be spent in music and singing, and the reading of the Harivansa, or Sánti parva of the Mahábhárata. The ceremony expiates all possible wickedness. The rite is held in little esteem, and is evidently compounded of the observances of various eras,—all of which are equally little understood,—although the compound is manifestly of a purificatory or expiatory character.

## Shat Tila Danam.

*Twenty-seventh Mágha, twelfth day of the light half* (*11th February*).—This may be considered as in some sort a continuation of the Bhaimyekádasí, and is intended for the same object —the removal or expiation of sin. As the name implies, six different acts are to be performed, in all which Tila, or sesamum seeds, are an essential ingredient. The person who observes the rite is to bathe in water in which they have been steeped—to anoint himself with a paste made of them—to offer them with clarified butter upon fire—to present them with water to the manes of his ancestors—to eat them—to give them away.† The consequences of so doing are purification from sin, exemption from sickness and misfortune, and a sojourn in Indra's heaven for

*[c. 65. See also Garudapurána, c. 127, quoted in the Sabdakalpadruma s. v. Bhaimí.]

† [Tithitattvam, quoted in the Sabdakalpadruma, p. 5655, a.]

thousands of years. According to the Brahma Purána, Yama, the deity of the infernal regions, created Sesamum after long and arduous penance upon this day, whence its sanctity. The same title and the same virtues are sometimes attributed also to the twelfth of the dark fortnight of the month, as was explained by Agastya to Dattátreya, when he asked by what means the effects of sin would be obviated, and sinners saved from hell without great effort or munificent donations.* The ceremonies to be performed with Tila seeds are the easy means of accomplishing the object. The importance attached to the use of Sesamum in most of the offerings, but especially in those to the Manes, is very remarkable and not very explicable. The legend of their being generated by Yama is rather the consequence than the cause of such appropriation. Sesamum seeds did form an ingredient in the offerings of the Greeks, but not with the same frequency, nor apparently with the same object. Cakes of sesamum were distributed by them at marriages, as the grains were considered typical of fertility. Perhaps some such opinion may have prevailed amongst the Hindus, and hence their use in obsequial offerings, the great end of which is not merely the satisfaction of the dead, but the perpetuation of progeny, and the prosperity of the living.

Another festival is observed on this day, in some parts of India, in honour of Vishnu, as the Varáha, his descent as a boar to lift up the earth from beneath the waters being supposed to have occurred on this day; hence it is termed also the Varáha Dwádasí.

## YUGADYA.

*Thirtieth Mágha, fifteenth day, light half, or full moon of Mágha (14th February).*—Bathing and fasting, and the offering of sesamum seeds to the Manes, are enjoined on the full moon of Mágha, and it is also held in additional honour as the anniversary of the commencement of the Kali Yug, or present age of the world, the age of impurity. According to some authorities the anniversaries of the Yugas occur not on the days of opposition, or full moon, but on those of conjunction or new moon, and this is more consonant to the character of the rites principally practised, as bathing and libations of water and sesamum to the Dii Manes. Thus the Vishnu Purána observes, the fifteenth of Mágha in the dark fortnight is one of the days called by ancient teachers the Anniversaries of the first day of a Yuga or Age, and are esteemed most sacred; on these days water mixed with sesamum seeds should be regularly presented to the progenitors of mankind; and

---

* Kalpa Druma.

again, the Pitris are described as saying, "After having received satisfaction for a twelvemonth, we shall further derive it from libations offered by our descendants at some holy place at the end of the dark fortnight of Mágha."

## SAKASHTAMI.

*Ninth of the solar month Phálguna; eighth day of lunar month Phálguna, dark half (22nd February).*—This is another of the eighth lunar days dedicated to the Manes or Pitris, when their worship is to be performed with the usual accompaniments of bathing and abstinence, and offerings to the Viswadevas or universal gods. On this occasion the offerings presented to the Pitris are, as the name imports, restricted to vegetable substances, Sáka signifying any potherb.

## VIJAYAIKADASI.

*Eleventh Phalguna, dark half (24th February).*—A celebration little known or observed. A water jar, decorated with the emblems of Vishnu, and considered as a type of him, is worshipped with the usual oblations; bathing in the morning and a vigil at night are to be observed. This is considered as a purificatory ceremony, first performed by Ráma to secure his passage across the ocean to Lanká: according to the authority, the Skanda Purána, quoted by the Kalpa Druma, it is an old ceremony of a purificatory tendency, removing sin and conducing to virtue.

Before taking leave of the period which has been latterly described, and which corresponds with the greater portion of the month of February, it is impossible not to be struck with the peculiar character of the ceremonies. From the time of the Vasantapanchamí, which ushers in the spring with indications of festivity, all the observances partake more or less of a lustral or purificatory purport; some of them have no other aim than the expiation of sin, whilst this in others is mixed up with the worship of the Manes. Purification from, or expiation of wickedness is, however, the predominating design of the ceremonies; and ablution and fasting, and abstinence of all kinds are the practices considered essential to the attainment of this object. Such are the chief intentions of the Makara Saptamí, Bhíshmáshtamí, Bhaimyekádasí, Shat-tila dánam, Yugádyá, and Sákáshtamí, all occurring within this interval. Now the spirit of the time is precisely that which marked a great part of the month of February among the Romans, and the name of the month itself is said to have been derived from its dedication by Numa to Februus, the god of lustrations, for in that month it was necessary to purify the city and pay to the Dii Manes the oblations that were their due: According to some, the name is derived from the verb "februor," to be cleansed or purified. The connexion between lustrations and obsequial rites is another analogy, and consonantly with this opinion, the Feralia, or worship of the manes were celebrated for several days in February, ending with the 17th, or according to some with the 23rd. The month was thence called also the *Feralis Mensis*. This similarity of time and of purposes can scarcely have been accidental, and there can be no reasonable doubt that the Feralia of the Romans and the Sráddha of the Hindus, the worship of the Pitris and of the Manes, have a common character and had a common origin.

## SIVA-RATRI.

*Fourteenth of the lunar month Phálguna; dark half (27th February)*.—This, in the estimation of the followers of Siva, is the most sacred of all their observances, expiating all sins, and securing the attainment of all desires during life, and union with Siva or final emancipation after death. The ceremony is said to have been enjoined by Siva himself, who declared to his wife Umá, that the fourteenth of Phálguna, if observed in honour of him, should be destructive of the consequences of all sin, and should confer final liberation. According to the Isána Sanhitá, it was on this day that Siva first manifested himself as a marvellous and interminable Linga, to confound the pretensions of both Brahmá and Vishnu, who were disputing which was the greater divinity. To decide the quarrel, they agreed that he should be acknowledged the greater, who should first ascertain the limits of the extraordinary object which appeared of a sudden before them. Setting off in opposite directions, Vishnu undertook to reach the base, Brahmá the summit; but after some thousand years of the gods spent in the attempt, the end seemed to be as remote as ever, and both returned discomfited and humiliated, and confessed the vast superiority of Siva. The legend seems to typify the exaltation of the Saiva worship over that of Vishnu and Brahmá, an event which no doubt at one time took place.

There is some difference of practice in respect to the day on which this festival is observed; according to some authorities, it is held on the fourteenth of the dark half of Mágha, according to others on the fourteenth of that of Phálguna; but this is a mere nominal difference, arising from the modes of reckoning the beginning of the month from the new or the full moon. Another difference, which is less easily adjusted, is that of date; some considering the festival as properly commencing on the thirteenth instead of the fourteenth; which appears to be the case in the South, according to the published calendars. This arises from the circumstance of the chief part of the ceremony being observed by night, as the name of Siva-rátri denotes, and of a variety in the apportionment of the hours of the night to the series of observances. According to some, the ceremony should begin on the evening of the thirteenth Tithi, or lunar day, if it extends to four hours after sunset; according to others, it should begin on whichever of the two tithis or lunar days comprises the larger proportion of the hours of the night; according to some, it should be held on the Tithi, which comprises both evening twilight, and midnight; and according to others, that which includes midnight without the evening. These are knotty points, which are not very intelligible without reference to an almanac, but they are not the less important in the eyes of the worshippers of Siva. When the Tithi coincides with the solar day, or lasts from sunrise, it is called Suddha, or pure, and the rite begins with the morning of the fourteenth and closes on the morning of the fifteenth.

The three essential observances are fasting during the whole Tithi, or lunar day, and holding a vigil and worshipping the Linga during the night; but the ritual is loaded with a vast number of directions, not only for the presentation of offerings of various kinds to the Linga, but for gesticulations to be employed, and prayers to be addressed to various subordinate divinities connected with Siva, and to Siva himself in a variety of forms. After bathing in the morning, the worshipper recites his Sankalpa, or pledges himself to celebrate the worship. He repeats the ablution in the evening, and going afterwards to a temple of Siva, renews his pledge, saying, "I will perform the worship of Siva, in the hope of accomplishing all my wishes, of obtaining long life, and progeny, and wealth, and for the expiation of all sins of whatever dye I may have committed during the past year, open or secret, knowingly or unknowingly, in thought, or act, or speech."* He then scatters mustard-seed with special mantras, and offers an argha; after which he goes through the mátriká nyása,—a set of gesticulations accompanied by short mystical prayers, consisting chiefly of unmeaning syllables, preceded by a letter of the alphabet: as, A-kam, A-srán, salutation to the thumb; I-chan, I-srín, salutation to the fore-finger; U-stan, U-stúm, salutation to the middle-finger; and so on, going through the whole of the alphabet with a salutation, or namaskár, to as many parts of the body, touching each in succession, and adding, as the Mantras proceed, names of the Mátris, female Saktis, or energies of Siva, who, by virtue of these incantations, are supposed to take up their abode for the time in the different members of the worshipper. Other objects are supposed to be effected by similar means; impediments are obviated by stamping thrice, and repeating as often the Mantra "Haun, to the weapon, phat;" next, with the

* [See Pránatoshaní, f. 173, b, 1.2.]

same mantra, and by thrice snapping the finger, the ten quarters of the sphere, or universal space, are aggregated in the Linga; and the purification of all beings is to be effected by thrice clapping the hands together, and uttering the same Mantra each time. The repetition of nyása, or touching parts of the body whilst repeating mystical ejaculations, accompanies every offering made to the Linga, as fruits, flowers, incense, lights, and the like, during the whole ceremony.

When the rite is performed, as it most usually is, in the performer's own residence, a Linga, if not already set up, is consecrated for the purpose; and this is to be propitiated with different articles in each watch of the night on which the vigil is held. In the first watch, it is to be bathed with milk, the worshipper, or the Brahman employed by him, uttering the Mantra "Haun—reverence to Isána." An offering is then made with the prayer: "Devoutly engaging in thy worship, oh Iswara, and in repeating thy names, I celebrate the Siva-rátri rite according to rule, do thou accept this offering!" Incense, fruits, flowers, and articles of food, as boiled rice, or sometimes even dressed flesh are offered with the customary prostration, and with the repetition of other Mantras.

A similar course is followed in the other three periods, with a modification of the formulæ, and the articles used to bathe the Linga with. Then in the second, it is bathed with curds, with the Mantra, "Haun—reverence to Aghora;" and the mantra of the Argha is "Reverence to the holy Siva, the destroyer of all sins; I offer this Argha at the Siva-rátri, do thou with Umá be propitious." In the third, the bathing is performed with ghee, with the Mantra "Haun, reverence to Vámadeva;" and the Argha-mantra is, "I am consumed by pain, poverty, and sorrow: oh Lord of Párvati, do thou, oh beloved of Umá, accept the Argha I present thee on this Siva-rátri!" In the fourth watch the Linga is bathed with honey, with the Mantra "Haun, reverence to Sadyojáta;" and the Argha-prayer is, "Oh Sankara! take away the many sins committed by me, accept, beloved of Umá, the oblation I present thee on this the night of Siva." At the end of the watch, or daylight, the ceremony is to be concluded with the radical mantra, "Siváya-namah", and some such prayers as these: "Through thy favour, oh Iswara! this rite is completed without impediment; oh look with favour, oh lord of the universe, Hara, sovereign of the three worlds, on what I have this day done, which is holy and dedicated to Rudra! Through thy grace has this rite been accomplished. Be propitious to me, oh thou most glorious! Grant to me increase of affluence: merely by beholding thee I am assuredly sanctified." Oblations to fire are then to be made, and the ceremony concludes with further offerings to the Linga, and with the Mantra,

"By this rite may Sankara be propitiated, and coming hither, bestow the eye of knowledge on him who is burnt up by the anguish of worldly existence." Brahmans are to be entertained, and presents are to be made to them by the master of the house and his family holding a feast.

Those modes of adoration which are at all times addressed to the different forms of Siva, and those articles which are peculiarly enjoined to be presented to the Linga, form, of course, part of the observances of the Siva-rátri. Amongst the forms is the Japa, or muttered recitation of his different names as the worshipper turns between his fingers the beads of a rosary, made of the seeds of the Rudráksha, or Eleocarpus. The fullest string contains one hundred and eight beads, for each of which there is a separate appellation, as Siva, Rudra, Hara, Sankara, Iswara, Maheswara, Súlapáni, Pasupati, and others. Amongst the latter are certain leaves and flowers, and fruits, and especially those of the bel-tree, as in the text—"The Vilwa is the granter of all desires, the remover of poverty; there is nothing with which Sankara is more gratified than with the leaf of the Vilwa." The flower of the Dhattúra is another of his favourites, and a single presentation of it to a Linga is said to secure equal recompense as the gift of a hundred thousand cows. At the Siva-rátri worship, the Linga may be crowned with a chaplet of Ketakí flowers, but only on this occasion. According to the legend, a Ketakí blossom fell from the top of the miraculous Siva-linga, already alluded to as having appeared to Brahmá and Vishnu, and being appealed to by the former, falsely affirmed that Brahmá had taken it from the summit of the Linga. Vishnu, knowing this to be untrue, pronounced an imprecation upon the flower, that it should never more be offered to Siva. He was moved, however, by the penitence of the flower, so far to remit the penalty, as to allow its decorating the Linga worshipped at the Siva-rátri pújá.

The worship of Siva at this season is permitted to all castes, even to Chandálás, and to women, and the use of the Mantras seems to be allowed to them; the only exception being the mystical syllable "Om." This they are not to utter; but they may go through the acts of worship with the prayer "Siváya namah." The same rewards attend their performance of it with faith, elevation to the sphere of Siva, identification with him and freedom from future birth, and these benefits accrue even though the rite be observed unintentionally and unwittingly, as is evidenced by the legend of a forester which is related in the second part of the Siva Purána, ch. XXXIV. Being benighted in the woods on the Siva-rátri, the forester took shelter in a Vilwa tree. Here he was kept in a state of perpetual wakefulness by dread of a tiger prowling round the foot of the tree. He therefore observed, though compulsorily, the Jágarana or vigil. The forester had nothing with him to eat, consequently he held the fast. Casting down the leaves of the tree to frighten the tiger, some of them fell upon a deserted Linga near the spot, and thus he made the prescribed offering. On the ensuing morning the forester fell a prey to the tiger, but such was the fruit of his involuntary observance of the rites of the Siva-rátri, that when the messengers of Yama came to take his spirit to the infernal regions they were opposed by the messengers of Siva, who enlisted him in their ranks, and carried him off in triumph to the heaven of their master.

Notwithstanding the reputed sanctity of the Siva-rátri, it is evidently of sectarial and comparatively modern, as well as merely local institution, and consequently offers no points of analogy to the practices of antiquity. It is said in the Kalpa Druma, that two of the mantras are from the Rig veda, but they are not cited, and it may well be doubted if any of the Vedas recognise any such worship of Siva. The great authorities for it are the Puránas and the Tantras; the former—the Siva, Linga, Padma, Matsya, and Váyu, are quoted chiefly for the general enunciations of the efficacy of the rite and the great rewards attending its performance: the latter for the mantras: the use of mystical formulæ, of mysterious letters and syllables, and the practice of the Nyása and other absurd gesticulations being derived mostly, if not exclusively, from them, as the Isána Sanhitá, the Siva Rahasya, the Rudra Yámala, Mantra-Mahodadhi, and other Tántrika works. The age of these compositions is unquestionably not very remote, and the ceremonies for which they are the only authorities, can have no claim to be considered as parts of the primitive system. This does not impair the popularity of the rite, and the importance attached to it is evidenced by the copious details which are given by the compilers of the Tithi Tattwa and Kalpa Druma regarding it, and by the manner in which it is observed in all parts of India.

The performance of the ceremonies of the Siva-rátri is possessed of enhanced efficacy when conducted at those places which are in an especial manner dedicated to Siva, particularly at the shrines which were known to have been celebrated seats of worship of the Linga before the Mohammedan invasion. Such is the temple of Vaidyanáth in Bengal, about 110 miles W. by N. from Murshedábád. The Linga worshipped there is one of the twelve great Lingas which were worshipped in India at least ten centuries ago, and still retains its reputation. In consequence of the establishment of the Mohammedan rule, and its position in a rugged and mountainous country overrun with thickets, the shrine fell for a season into neglect and decay, but it was repaired and restored to popularity by a Maithila Brahman about two centuries since. An annual Melá takes place at Vaidyanáth,* at the

* [Sivapurána, c. 55.]

Siva-rátri, when more than a hundred thousand pilgrims assemble. The meeting lasts three days, and the offerings made to the temple ordinarily exceed a lakh and a-half of rupees. The shrine has some credit as an oracle, and a course of worship and fasting on the spot is productive of dreams, which are believed to convey the answers of Siva to the prayers and petitions that have been preferred to him.

A still more numerous concourse of pilgrims occurs annually on the Siva-rátri at the temple of Mallikárjuna* in the Dekhan, also one of the twelve ancient Lingas, the temple of which is situated in a country quite as difficult of access as Vaidyanáth. An account of the Melá held here is given by the late Colonel Mackenzie, in the fifth volume of the Asiatic Researches. He calls the place Srí-parvatham—properly Srí Parvata, or Srí Saila, the holy mountain—he specifies the name of the Linga, however, as Mallikarja, that is to say Mallikárjuna.

According to the Bombay Calendar, there is a numerous assemblage of Hindus at the Siva-rátri on the Island of Elephanta, the great cave temple of which place contains the well known three-headed image of Siva.

## Govinda Dwadasi.

*Twenty-seventh solar Phálguna ; twelfth day, light half (13th March)*.—This is a festival, which, as observed in Bengal, is held in honour of Krishna, who is worshipped in his juvenile form as a cowherd. In Hindustan it is termed the Nrisinha dwádasí, and is dedicated to Vishnu in his Avatára of the Nrisinha, or man-lion. In neither is it an observance held in much repute.†

## Ghanta-karna Puja.

*Twenty-ninth solar Phálguna ; fourteenth day, light half (14th March)*.—This is also a minor festival, and apparently confined to Bengal. Ghantá-karna, one of Siva's ganas, or attendants, is to be worshipped under the type of a water-jar : the object of the rite is expressed in this prayer, which accompanies the presentation of fruits and flowers to the jar: "Oh Ghantá-karna! healer of diseases, do thou preserve me from the fear of cutaneous affections." Ghantá-karna is described in the Siva Purána as endowed with great personal beauty, and is, therefore, reputed to sympathise with those who suffer any disfigurement. In Hindustan there are directions for worshipping Maheswara, or Siva himself, on the fourteenth of the light half of Phálguna.

---

* [Sivapurána, c. 44.]

† [Bhavishyottarapurána, c. 67.]

## Dola Yatra, or Holi.

*Thirtieth solar Phálguna, or first of Chaitra ; fifteenth day, light half, or full moon of Phálguna (16th March).*—Although named together, and in various parts of India, especially in Bengal, confounded with each other, yet in other places these festivals are still, as they no doubt were originally elsewhere, distinct;* the Dolatsava, or Swinging Festival taking place at a date something later, and this period belonging, most appropriately, to the Holí. It will be convenient to notice them here together, however, for the Holí, as a distinct celebration, is not known in Bengal, although many of the observances which are there practised at the Dola Yátrá are in many respects the same, are influenced by the same spirit, and express in the like style of language and deportment the feelings of exuberant gladness which hail the return of spring.

When India was governed by native princes, and the institutions of the Hindus were in full vigour, there is reason to believe, that at this time of the year a series of connected and consistent festivities spread through a protracted period of several weeks, and that the whole constituted the Vasantotsava, the feast of Vasanta or Spring. The proper commencement of this period was, perhaps, the Vasanta Panchamí, the fifth of the light half of Mágha, which, as we have had occasion to notice, was regarded as the beginning of Spring. After this, however, ensued the gloomy succession of lustral and purificatory rites which have been described, and which suspend the season of festivity until the period now under consideration, when the Holí takes the place of the initiatory Vasanta Panchamí, and is followed by celebrations in honour of Spring, and the friend of Spring, Love. Whether there has been any dislocation of times and observances here—whether the lustral days did not at one time precede the vernal rejoicings, we have no means of determining; but it is somewhat remarkable, that such was the case with the February of the Romans, which, in the days of Numa, when their year consisted of but ten months, was the last of the year, and therefore, was fitly enough the season for expiating the accumulated iniquities of the preceding months. However this may be, such is now the case, and the vernal festival is broken in upon and interrupted by observances of a different complexion—the effect of which may, perhaps, have been to heighten by the contrast the sense of exhilaration when the time for it recurred.

It is also to be remarked, that although traces of the original purport of the festival are palpable enough, yet that Love and

* The Kalpa Druma does notice a Dolatsava,—the swinging of Krishna on the Phálguná purnimá.

Spring have been almost universally deposed from the rites over which they once presided, and that they have been superseded by new and less agreeable mythological creations; new legends have also been invented to account for the origin and object of the celebration, having little or no obvious relation to the practices which are pursued. Thus, in Bengal, the divinity worshipped at the Dola Yátrá is the juvenile Krishna, whilst in Hindustan the personified Holí is a female hobgoblin, a devourer of little children.

As publicly commemorated in Bengal, the Dola Yátrá, or swinging festival, begins on the fourteenth day of the light half of Phálguna (about the middle of March). The head of the family fasts during that day. In the evening fire-worship is performed; after which the officiating Brahman sprinkles upon an image of Krishna, consecrated for the occasion, a little red powder, and distributes a quantity of the same among the persons present. This powder, termed Phalgu, or Abíra, is made chiefly of the dried and pounded root of the Curcuma Zerumbet, or of the wood of the Cæsalpinia Sappan, which are of a red colour, or in some places the yellow powder of Turmeric is substituted. After this ceremony is concluded a bonfire is made on a spot previously prepared, and a sort of Guy Fawkes-like effigy, termed Holiká, made of bamboo laths and straw, is formally carried to it and committed to the flames. In villages and small towns the bonfire is public, and is made outside the houses. The figure is conveyed to the spot by Brahmans or Vaishnavas, in regular procession, attended by musicians and singers. Upon their arrival at the spot, the image is placed in the centre of the pile, and the ministering Brahman, having circumambulated it seven times, sets it on fire. The assistants should then immediately return to their homes. The remainder of the day is passed in merriment and feasting.

Before daylight on the morning of the fifteenth, the image of Krishna is carried to the swing, which has been previously set up, and placed in the seat or cradle, which, as soon as the dawn appears, is set gently in motion for a few turns. This is repeated at noon, and again at sunset During the day, the members of the family and their visitors, who are numerous on this occasion, amuse themselves by scattering handfuls of red powder over one another, or by sprinkling each other with rose-water, either plain or similarly tinted. The place where the swing is erected is the usual site of the sport, and continues so for several days. Boys and persons of the lower orders sally forth into the streets and throw the powder over the passengers, or wet them with the red liquid thrown through syringes, using, at the same time, abusive and obscene language. In the villages, the men generally take part in the mischief, and persons of respectability and females are encountered with gross expressions, or sometimes with rough usage, and rarely, therefore, trust themselves out of their houses whilst the license continues.

The people of Orissa have no bonfire at the Dola Yatra, but they observe the swinging and the scattering of the abira; they have also some peculiar usages. Their Gosáins, Brahmans, followers of Chaitanya, carry in procession the images of the youthful Krishna to the houses of their disciples and their patrons, to whom they present some of the red powder and atr of roses, and receive presents of money and cloth in return.

The caste of Gopas, or cowherds, is everywhere prominently conspicuous in this ceremony, and especially so amongst the Uriyas; and at the Dola Yátrá, or Holi, they not only renew their own garments, but all the harness and equipments of their cattle; they also bathe them and paint their foreheads with sandal and turmeric. They themselves collect in parties, each under a leader or choragus, whom they follow through the streets, singing, and dancing, and leaping, as if wild with joy. A curious part of their proceeding, suggesting analogies, possibly accidental, with some almost obsolete usages amongst ourselves, is their being armed with slender wands; and as they go along, the leader every now and then halts and turns round to his followers, and the whole clatter their wands together for an instant or two, when they resume their route, repeating their vociferations and songs, chiefly in praise of Krishna or in commemoration of his juvenile pastimes.

Although the Holi is considered in some parts of Hindustan to begin with the vernal fifth, or Vasanta Panchamí, yet the actual celebration of it, even in Upper India, does not take place till about ten days before the full moon of Phálguna. The two first days of this term are of preparation merely; new garments, red or yellow, are put on, and families feast and make merry together; on the eighth day, the work proceeds more in earnest: images of Krishna are set up and worshipped, and smeared with red powder, or sprinkled with water, coloured with the same material. In the villages and towns, where there is no Anglo-Indian police to interfere, the people, having selected an open spot in the vicinity, bring thither gradually the materials of a bonfire,—wood, grass, cow-dung, and other fuel. The head men of the villages, or the chiefs of the trades, first contribute their quotas; the rest collect whatever they can lay hands upon,—fences, door-posts, and even furniture, if not vigilantly protected. If these things be once added to the pile, the owner cannot reclaim them, and it is a point of honour to acquiesce—any measures, however, are allowable to prevent their being carried off. During the whole period, up to the fifteenth day, the people go about scattering the powder and red liquid over each other, singing and dancing, and annoying passengers by mischievous tricks, practical jokes, coarse witticisms, and vulgar abuse. In the larger towns, which are subject to British authority, the festival is restricted to three days, and the celebrants are not permitted to attack indifferent passers-by of any degree. In Calcutta little of the festival is witnessed, except among the palankin bearers, who are generally permitted by their masters to devote a few hours of the forenoon, for two or three days, to amuse themselves by staining each others' faces and clothes, and singing and dancing, and sometimes getting tipsy. They do not venture to throw the powder over their masters, but they bring a small quantity with some sweetmeats on a tray, and the courtesy is acknowledged by those who do not despise national observances and the merry-making of their dependants by placing two or three rupees upon the platter. In the native regiments a little more license is allowed, and the officers are gently bepowdered with the abíra; and at the Courts of Hindu princes, when such things were, the British Resident and the officers of his suite were usually participators in the public diversions of their Highnesses. An amusing account of the proceedings at the Court of Maháráj Dowlat Rao Sindhia is given by Major Broughton, in his letter from a Marhatta camp.

We have, however, in this digression rather anticipated matters, and must return to the fourteenth day, by which time the pile of the bonfire is completed. It is then consecrated and lighted up by a Brahman, and when the flames break forth, the spectators crowd round it to warm themselves, an act that is supposed to avert ill-luck for the rest of the year; they engage also in some rough gambols, trying to push each other nearer to the fire than is agreeable or safe, and as the blaze declines, jump over and toss about the burning embers; when the fuel is expended and the fire extinct, which is not until the fifteenth or full moon, the ashes are collected and thrown into the water. Such of the celebrants as are Saivas take up part and smear their bodies over with them in imitation of Siva. According to Colonel Tod, the practice of the Rájputs conforms so far to the original institution, that for forty days after the Vasanta Panchamí, or up to the full moon of Phálguna, the utmost license prevails at Udaypur, both in word and action; the lower classes regale on stimulating confections and intoxicating liquors, and even respectable persons roam about the streets like bacchanals, vociferating songs in praise of the powers of nature. The chief orgies, however, take place after the beginning of Phálguna, when the people are continually patrolling the streets, throwing the common powder at each other or ejecting a solution of it from syringes, until their clothes and countenances are all of the same dye. A characteristic mode of keeping the festival is playing the Holi on horseback, when the riders pelt each other with balls of the red powder, inclosed in thin plates of talc which break when they strike.

On the full moon, or Púrnimá, the Ráná goes in state to an open pavilion in the centre of a spacious plain, where he is attended by his chiefs, and passes an hour listening to the Holi songs. The surrounding crowd amuse themselves with throwing the red powder on all within their reach. After this, the Ráná feasts his chiefs, and presents them with cocoa-nuts and swords of lath, in burlesque of real swords; "in unison," Tod observes, "with the character of the day, when war is banished, and the multiplication not the destruction of man is the behest of the goddess who rules the Spring." At nightfall the forty days conclude with the burning of the Holi, when they light large fires into which various substances as well as the abira are cast, and around which groups of children are dancing and screaming in the streets. The sports continue till three hours after sunrise, when the people bathe, change their garments, worship and return to the state of sober citizens; and princes and chiefs receive gifts from their domestics.

Amongst the Tamils, or people of Madras and the farther south, the Dolotsava, or Swing festival, does not occur until about a month later; but on the fifteenth of Phálguna they have a celebration more analogous to the Holi of Hindustan, and which is no doubt a genuine fragment of the primitive institution, the adoration of the personified Spring as the friend and associate of the deity of Love. The festival of the full moon of Phálguna is the Káma-dahanam, the burning of Kámadeva, whose effigy is committed to the flames. This is supposed to commemorate the legend of Káma's having been consumed by the flames which flashed indignant from the eye of Siva, when the archer god presumed to direct his shaft against the stern deity, and inflame his breast with passion for Párvati, the daughter of the monarch of the Himálaya Mountains. Kámadeva was reduced to a heap of ashes, although he was afterwards restored to existence by the intercession of the bride of Mahádeva. The bonfires in the Dekhan are usually made in front of the temples of Siva, or sometimes of Vishnu, at midnight, and when extinct the ashes are distributed amongst the assistants, who rub them over their persons. The scattering of the abira, the singing and abuse, and the ordinary practices of the festival in Upper India, are also in use in the South.

The prominence given to Kámadeva at this season by the Tamil races, and their preserving some remnant of the purport of the primitive festival, are the more interesting, that little or no trace of the chief object of worship is preserved in Upper India. Kámadeva and Vasanta are quite out of date, and legends of a totally different tendency have been devised to explain the purpose of the bonfire and the effigy exposed to it. The heroine of these legends is a malignant witch, or a foul female goblin, or Rákshasí, named Horí, Holí, or Holiká, a word which, although it occurs in some of the Puránas, is not of a very obvious Sanskrit etymology.*

According to one account Holi is the same as the female demon Pútaná, of whom it is related in the Vishnu and Bhágavata Puránas,† and in the popular biographies of Krishna taken from them, that she attempted to destroy the baby Krishna, by giving him her poisoned nipples to suck. The little god, knowing with whom he had to deal, sucked so hard and perseveringly, that he drained the Rákshasí of her life. The popular legend adds, that the dead body disappeared, and the Gopas, or cowherds of Mathurá, burnt the Rákshasí therefore in effigy. The chief authority for the institution of the Holí, however, is the Bhavishyottara Purána,‡ and as an authentic representation of the popular notion which now prevails, and which is nevertheless no doubt erroneous, I shall give a translation of the legend told in that compilation.

"Yudhishthira said, 'Tell me, Janárdana, wherefore on the full moon of Phálguna, a festival is celebrated in the world, in every village, and in every town; why are children playing and dancing in every house, why is the Holiká lighted, what words are uttered, what is the meaning of the name Attátajá, what of Síloshná, what divinity is worshipped at this season, by whom was the rite instituted, what observances are to be practised? Give me, Krishna, a full account of these things.' Krishna replied: 'In the Krita age, Yudhishthira, there was a king named Raghu, a brave warrior, endowed with all good qualities, a kind speaker, and deeply read in the Vedas; he had subdued the whole earth, had brought all its princes under his authority, and virtuously cherished his subjects, as if they had been his own children. In his reign there was neither famine, nor sickness, nor untimely death, nor any iniquity, nor departure from the precepts of religion. Whilst he was thus governing his kingdom, agreeably to the duties of his regal caste, all his people came to him and called upon him to preserve them. They said, 'Lo, into our houses a female Rákshasí named Dundhá enters, both by day and by night, and forcibly afflicts our children, and she cannot be driven out either by charmed bracelets, or by water, or by seeds of mustard, or by holy teachers skilful in exorcismus. Such, oh king! as we have related, is the story of Dundha.'

* It appears from the Bhavishyottara Purána, as given below, to be derived from Homa, burnt offering, and Loka, mankind, because the latter are made prosperous by the performance of the former on this occasion: an evidently fanciful derivation.

† [V. P. V. 5. Bhág. P. X. 4. Harivansa, 3423 ff.]  ‡ [c. 117.]

"When the king heard these things, he consulted the Muni Narada. The Muni replied: 'I will tell you by what means the fiend is to be destroyed. This day is the fifteenth of the light fortnight of Phálguna; the cold season has departed, the warm weather will commence with dawn. Chief of men! let the assurance of safety be this day given to your people, and let them, freed from terror, laugh and sport; let the children go forth rejoicing, like soldiers delighted to go to battle, equipped with wooden swords. Let also a pile of dry wood and stones be prepared, and let it be lighted according to rule, while incantations are recited destructive of wicked fiends. Then let the people, fearless, thrice circumambulate the fire, exclaiming, 'Kila, kila!' and clapping their hands; and let them sing and laugh, and let every one utter, without fear, whatever comes into his mind. In various ways, and in their own speech, let them freely indulge their tongues, and sing and sing again a thousand times, whatever songs they will. Appalled by those vociferations, by the oblation to fire, and by the loud laughter (attahása) of the children, that wicked Rákshasí shall be destroyed, and thenceforth the festival of the Holiká shall be renowned among mankind. Inasmuch as the oblation to fire (homa), offered by the Brahmans upon this day, effaces sin and confers peace upon the world (loka), therefore shall the day be called the Holiká; and inasmuch as the day of full moon comprises the essence of all lunations, so from its intrinsic excellence is Phálguna the bestower of universal happiness. On this day, upon the approach of evening, children should be detained at home; and into the court-yard of the house, smeared with cow-dung, let the master of the house invite many men, mostly youths, having wooden swords in their hands: with these they shall touch the children, with songs and laughter, and thus preserving them, shall be entertained with boiled rice and sugar. Thus Dundhá is to be got rid of at the hour of sunset, and by this means the safety of children is ensured on the approach of night.'"

The same authority describes a domestic ceremony to be held on the following morning, when offerings are to be made to a water-jar, as a type of Vishnu; and presents are to be given to bards, singers, and Brahmans. The observance of this secures the enjoyment of all desires, and the continuation of life, wealth, and posterity.

Of the songs that are sung at this season, the character is generally said to be highly exceptionable. All that I have had an opportunity of seeing are characterised by little else than insipidity; they are short, seldom exceeding two or three stanzas, the first of which is repeated as a sort of refrain or burden, and the whole song is sung da capo, over and over again. They are either praises of the month or allusions to the juvenile Krishna, in connexion with the festival, and are supposed to be uttered by the female companions of his boyish frolics in Vrindávana. The following are a few of them:

I.

"Oh friend! proud as you are of your youth, be careful of your garments The month of Phálguna fills with grief those whose lovers are far away. Oh friend! proud as you are of your youth," &c.

II.

"The month of Phálguna has arrived; I shall mingle with the crowd, and partake of the sports of the Hori. Oh friend! an hour of pleasure is worth a night of mortification. The month of Phálguna has arrived," &c.

III.

"I met on my way the lord of Vrindávana: how can I go to fetch water? If I ascend the roof, he pelts me with pellets of clay; if I go to the river, he sprinkles me over with red powder; if I repair to Gokul, he showers upon me tinted dust. Thus he drives me distracted. I met in the way the lord of Vrindávana."

IV.

"My beloved has sent me a letter to summon his bride home; I blush for my unworthiness. How can I repair to one who knows my imperfections? I blush for my unworthiness. The litter is prepared, but no female friend accompanies me. I blush for my unworthiness, now that my lover summons me home."

V.

"My boddice is wet through; who has thrown the tinted liquor upon me? It is Kanhaiyá, the son of Nanda. It is the month of Phálguna. My boddice is wet through," &c.

VI.

"Oh lord of Vraj! gaily you sport to the merry sound of the tabor, and dance along with the nymphs of Vrindávana. Oh lord of Vraj!" &c.

The deviation from ancient times and practices which marks the recurrence of the Vernal Festival among the Hindus themselves, renders it far from surprising that we should fail to find an exact accordance, in all respects, between the Indian observance, as now followed, and that which has prevailed in other seasons and places, with respect to celebrations, the general purport and character of which present probable analogies. We have no right to look for a minute agreement, but it can scarcely be doubted, that there were festivals among the Romans, and that there are even yet observances in Europe which express a similar intention, and originated in the same feelings, and which are, possibly, as well as the Hindu Holí, reliques of what was once the universal method adopted by mankind to typify the genial influence of Spring upon both the inanimate and animated creation, and to express the passionate feelings inspired by the season, and the delight which the revival of nature diffused.

There is another of the usages of the Holí which finds a parallel in modern times, although at a somewhat later period. It is mentioned by Colonel Pearce, that one subject of diversion during the Holí, is to send people on errands and expeditions that are to end in disappointment, and raise a laugh at the expense of the person sent. He adds that, Suraj-ad-daula, the Nawáb of Bengal, of Black Hole celebrity, was very fond of making Holí Fools.* The identity of this practice with making April Fools as noticed by Colonel Pearce, is concurred in by Maurice, who remarks, "that the boundless hilarity and jocund sports, prevalent on the 1st day of April in England, and during the Holí Festival in India, have their origin in the ancient practice of celebrating, with festival rites, the period of the vernal equinox, when the new year of Persia anciently began."

## Additional Remarks on the Holi.

To the foregoing account of Wilson, the following details may be added:

A Calcutta account of Hindu Festivals says that the "Dola or Swinging Festival is in commemoration of the sports of Krishna and his mistress Rádhá, who, on this day, tradition says, amused themselves with rocking and throwing red powder at each other.

"On the night before the worship, fireworks are let off, dances with most immodest gestures take place, and indecent songs are sung; after which, towards morning, Krishna and Rádhá are placed on a chair suspended by ropes in the form of a swing, and then rocked, amidst music, shouts, laughter, and frantic expressions of all kinds; old, grey-headed men taking as active a part in their fooleries as the most giddy and thoughtless youth.

"During the day, the worshippers wander about the streets, throwing red powder (*Phágu*) at the passengers, with their hands, or through a syringe, in imitation of the god, who himself, when incarnate, took a particular pleasure in this sport."

* Asiatic Researches, Vol. II., p. 334.

Mr. B. M. Malabari well calls this festival the "unholy Holi." He thus describes it even in Bombay:

"In the streets you may still encounter respectable Vaishnava merchants pelting each other; but the wild delirium excited by the festival is best seen among the Marwaris.

"Here a crowd of these *bhang* intoxicated bacchanals will besiege a neighbouring Zenana, by way of seranade, I suppose, and shout their rude amorous ditties with significant gestures and attitude. The filthy epithets, the wanton glances, the obscene gestures, defy description; but these are rewarded, on the part of the Marwaran (females) by equally shameless retorts and the squirts of red paint."*

Pandit Natesa Sastri, gives the following explanations of the use of obscene language at the festival:

"There was a very wicked female demon, named Holika, who every day visited some town to carry away children to feast on them. When a complaint was made to the king of the Rákshasas, he ordered that t' people should give her one child a day. One day it fell to the lot of ı old woman to give up her grandson, her only surviving relation. When an old mendicant heard the moanings of the old woman, he told her how the demon Holika might be destroyed. If she hears obscene abuse, she will fall down and die. All the children of the village should go out to meet Holika, using obscene language and making obscene gestures. The children did so; she died, and they cremated her body. The Holi feast of the Hindus originates from this legend."†

It has been said of the Holi that "*obscenity is the measure of piety.*"

Happily among educated Hindus there is a growing feeling against such abominations. The *Indu Prakash*, referring to the Holi, says:

"We think that committees ought to be formed in every place for the purpose of putting down the evil by prosecuting those who use obscene language in public. Our Municipal Boards and Commissioners could do much in the matter."

In the Panjab a harmless festival, called the *Pavitra Holi*, has been sought to be substituted.

Such efforts deserve every encouragement.

## BURWA MANGAL.

On the first Tuesday‡ after the Holi, a supplementary repetition of it is held at Benares, with sundry modifications of a not uninteresting description. An account of the festival has been given by the late Mr. J. Prinsep, in his valuable views

* *Gujarat and the Gujaratis*, pp. 350, 351.

† *Hindu Feasts, Fasts, and Ceremonies*, abridged, pp. 48, 14.

‡ Hence its name Mangal.

of Benares, and I had also an opportunity of witnessing its observance. During the day the people go in crowds to a place called Durgá kunda, a large tank and temple dedicated to Durgá, who is worshipped on this occasion. Although there are no regular processions, yet horses and elephants, gaily caparisoned, are plentifully scattered amongst the throng, and the garden walls along the road are crowded with spectators. Strolling actors, disguised as religious mendicants, or as individuals of inferior caste, both male and female, mingle with the crowd, and divert them with singing and dancing and absurd buffoonery. Sometimes different parties oppose each other in a contest of poetical improvisation. In the evening, the more opulent inhabitants of Benares embark on board boats fitted up for the occasion with platforms and awnings, and parade up and down the river throughout the night, having with them bands of musicians, and singers, and dancing girls. When the evening is advanced, the pinnace of the Rájá of Benares moves from his residence at Rámnagar, and slowly descends the stream, followed by other boats, lighted up, and displaying fireworks from time to time, until they take their station off one of the principal ghâts. The boats on the river are also illuminated, and are rowed up and down the stream, accompanied by numerous lesser craft selling refreshments, or bearing less wealthy amateurs to catch the strains of some popular songstress. The shore is thronged with people, and discharges of fireworks, with the river pageantry, amuse them until the end of the night. At day-break they are again clustered along the magnificent ghâts of Benares, and by their numbers, their order, their diversified and many-tinted costumes, in harmony with the elegant architecture of the surrounding edifices, the broad river, and the unclouded sky, present a picture of singular richness, gracefulness, animation, and beauty.

Upon the occasion on which I witnessed this festival, the Rájá, on the morning, received the visits of the Governor-General's agent, Mr. Brooke, and other European gentlemen of the station. They were entertained as usual with náching, but upon taking leave, in addition to the ordinary aspersion of rose-water, which was bestowed so copiously as to amount to a ducking, guests were pelted with rose-leaves, immense trays of which were brought in for the purpose. The attack was retaliated by a shower of the same missiles, which have at least the character of greater refinement than the confitti di gesso, the plaster of Paris pellets of the Carnival.

According to Mr. Prinsep, the ceremony originated with Zemindár Balwant Sing, the father of Raja Chait Sing, who adopted the celebration of the Holí on the river, for the gratification of Mír Rustam Ali, the Mohammedan Governor of the province, who had a house on the river-side. As he observes, however, the name Búrwa, old, indicates higher antiquity.

## Ghentu Puja.

*March.*

This is a Bengali festival held on the last day of Phálguna (February and March). Ghentu is an inferior deity, the god of itch and other skin diseases. Crookes gives the following account of the festival:

"The scene of the service is a dunghill. A broken earthenware pot, the bottom blackened by constant use for cooking, daubed white with lime, interspersed with a few streaks of turmeric, together with a bunch or two of the *ghentu* plant, and last not least, a broomstick of the genuine palmyra or cocoanut stock, serve as the representation of the presiding deity of itch The mistress of the family, for whose benefit the work is done, acts as priestess. After a few doggerel lines are recited, the pot is broken and the pieces collected by the children, who sing songs about the itch godling."*

## Baruni.

*March.*

This is a bathing festival, and takes place on the 13th day of the decrease of the moon in the month Chaitra (March—April). When it falls on a Saturday, and the star *Sota Bhissa*† is then on the meridian, it is called *Mahá Báruni;* and again, if the star *Shuba Jug* is in conjunction with *Sota Bhissa*, it is called *Mahá Maha Báruni.*

The benefits of bathing in the Ganges at the *Báruni* are equal to those resulting from bathing in that river at the time of 100 sun eclipses; the fruits of bathing at the *Mahá Báruni* equal to those of bathing at a million of sun eclipses; and those of bathing at the *Mahá Mahá Báruni* are so great, that three millions of generations of the ancestors of the bather are saved from hell by this single act of piety of their progeny.

At these bathing festivals, the natives from the remotest parts of Bengal, and even Orissa, proceed to the Ganges to perform their ablutions. Tribeni, six miles above Chinsurah, is especially resorted to by immense crowds; that place being held very sacred on account of the supposed junction of three rivers, and called for that reason by the natives the 'little *Prayág*' [Allahabad].

---

* *Popular Religion, etc., of Northern India*, p. 87.

† Á Aquarii.

## Ashok Shashti.

### *March.*

*Ashok Shashti* means 'Shashti the destroyer of sorrow.' It is held on the 12th of Chaitra. Those women who have children attend to this pújá to obtain the protection of the goddess *Shashti* on their offspring, and also to be delivered from all domestic troubles and evils.

Wilkins gives the following account of the goddess:

"Shashti, the goddess who rules over women and the protector of children, is regularly worshipped at six seasons of the year and at special seasons also. At child-birth, and even before, her blessing is invoked; and after birth until the child attains to manhood or womanhood, it is supposed to be under her special care. In the sickness of children her aid is first invoked to effect their recovery. At this festival it is not common to set up an image of the goddess; but as the banyan tree is regarded as specially sacred to her, she is represented by it on this occasion. On the day of worship the women of the neighbourhood march with music playing to the tree; the mothers of sons with joy written on their faces, those as yet unblessed with disappointment in their looks and fervent prayers for this blessing in their hearts and even on their lips. The mantras are recited by the priests; the honoured mothers who have sons give presents to those who have none, and the procession wends its way back to the village.

After this is over sons-in-law are invited to the houses of their fathers-in-law, and after being hospitably entertained there, are sent home laden with presents. On the whole, it is one of the happiest days of the year."*

Shashti is represented as a golden-complexioned woman, with a child in her arms, riding upon a cat. Hence no Hindu woman would under any circumstances injure that animal lest she should offend the goddess and be made to suffer for it. The ordinary representation of Shashti is a stone about the size of a man's head, placed under a banyan tree, which is decorated with flowers, and offerings of rice, fruits, &c., are made to it.†

## BASANTI PUJA.

### *About March 26th.*

*Básanti* is a name of *Durga*. The worship, which commences on the 7th of the increase of the moon Chaitra (March—April) lasts four days. The same ceremonies are gone through, and for the same purposes as at the grand festival in October, but not with such pomp and universality.

## SRI RAMA-NAVAMI.

### *About March 28th.*

SRI RAMA-NAVAMI from *Ram*, the 7th incarnation of Vishnu, and *Navami*, the 9th day of Chaitra Shuddh. On this day, it is said, Ramachandra, the 7th incarnation of Vishnu, was born at Ayodhya in Oudh, about B.C. 1400. It is celebrated from the 1st of Chaitra Shuddh to the 9th. The object of the incarnation, it is said, was to effect the destruction of Rawan, the ten-headed tyrant of Lanka or Ceylon, which was at last done with the assistance of Hanuman, the chief of the monkey tribe. On the first day, the temples of Rama are whitewashed, and illuminated in the evening, and the image of Rama is adorned with costly ornaments. In the evening the "Ramayana," or legendary history of Rama, is read in the temples, and in the night "Kirtan" is preached by the "Haridas," who describes the so-called morality and heroic actions of Rama. The red powder, called *gulal* (composed of barley meal or rice paste, or the *Trapa natans*, dyed with *bakam* or sapan wood) is thrown about. Nautches are not omitted during the nights. In some temples Brahmins are fed with rich and substantial dinners for eight successive days; these days are called Rama Navaratra, or nine nights of Rama. Many Hindus, both male and female, go to the temples of Rama to hear the Kirtan and Purána. The last or principal day is Rama-navami, when, it is said, Rama became incarnate at noon. In honour of this incarnation, some Hindus fast the whole day. They get up in the morning, wash themselves, and put

* *Modern Hinduism*, pp. 221, 222.

† Ward's *Hindus*, ii. 143.

on rich clothes and ornaments, and repair to the temples of Rama at about nine o'clock. Every temple of Rama is well furnished on this day, and the images are decorated with precious ornaments and rich brocade. A Haridas is engaged to describe the birth and circumstances that attend his incarnation. He continues his discourse till twelve o'clock, when he brings a small image of Rama, nicely ornamented and well clad, and shows it to his audience, telling them that it is Rama who became incarnate; he then puts it into a small cradle prepared for the purpose. The assembly then throw themselves prostrate before the image and worship it. Great is the rejoicing and acclamation on this occasion; they fling gulal on each other; and with great mirth, at about one o'clock, they go home, to return to the temples in the evening. The feast of Rama-navami is more particularly observed by the votaries of Vishnu.*

## Charak (Wheel) Puja.

*About the end of March.*

"It is said that an ancient king, by reason of his great austerities, obtained an interview with Siva, in commemoration of which this festival is held. The peculiarity of the worship consists in the fact that the devotees of Siva belonging to the lower castes assume the profession and dress of Sannyásis for a week or ten days, and march about the streets soliciting alms from people."†

It is held on the 28th, 29th, 30th, and 31st days of Chaitra, but, those persons who wish to be very meritorious on this occasion, prepare themselves, during the whole month of Chaitra by performing various ceremonies, and abstaining from different kinds of food, from spices, common salt, oil, and other gratifications, and by sleeping on coarse blankets, or on rushes.

Bráhmans, Khettriyás, and Vaishyás take no share in this festival except as spectators. The celebration of it is confined to the Sudrás, and even among them, only the very lowest classes take an active part in it. However, the Káyastas, writer caste, and other respectable Sudrás, often hire individuals from the dregs of the population, to act on their behalf, and to inflict the usual cruelties on themselves; but reserving of course for their own benefit the merit accruing from these practices. The Sudras who perform those penances *on their own account*, do it generally to fulfil a vow, which when sick, or suffering under any other calamity, either they themselves, or their relations on their behalf, had made. During the month of Chaitra, all these Sannyásis, although Sudras, wear the *paitá* or sacred thread, in the manner the Bráhmans do.

---

* Madras Almanac, also Bombay Almanac.

† Wilkins' *Modern Hinduism*, p. 285.

On the *first* day of the festival, the Sannyásis keep a partial fast, which consists in their eating only such food as has been cooked in *one* pot at the same time.

On the *second* day, which is called the *fruit day*, Phalerdin, the Sannyásis assemble in great numbers, and wander from village to village, begging from the inhabitants whatever fruits may be in season; and when they have gathered a great quantity, they deposit them in the temple of Siva. In the afternoon, they go about in the same manner, begging fire-wood, and collect it in an immense heap opposite to Sivá's temple. They then assemble on that spot, and regale themselves with the fruits that were presented to them in the morning; but perfect silence is required to reign at this meal, and if any human voice is heard, all eating must directly cease. In order therefore to avoid such a disastrous consequence, they take care to continue striking a gong, whose sound is sure to drown any voice that perchance might be uttered among them, or in the neighbourhood. Bundles of thorns are subsequently placed before the temple, and the Sannyásis cast themselves on them; and to bring the matter to a close, fire is put to the pile, which soon blazes briskly, after which the Sannyásis scatter the embers about, dance over them, and throw them in the air, or at each other.

The *third* day, early, the work of piercing the tongues and sides commences. At Calcutta, this is done at the celebrated temple of *Káli-ghát*, to which immense crowds resort, having with them drums and other instruments of music, and also spits, canes, ramrods, and different other articles, to pass through their tongues or sides. Some, with tinkling rings on their ankles, are dancing in a most frantic way, and exhibiting the most indecent gestures; whilst others are rending the air with their shouts and filthy songs. Arrived at *Káli-ghát*, they proceed to the great temple, where several blacksmiths are in attendance, ready, for a trifling fee, to pierce their tongues, cut their sides, or perform any operation the Sannyásis may desire. They then thrust through their pierced tongues, spears, swords, bambus, hukah-tubes, &c., and through their sides, ropes, the ends of which two persons hold before and behind; whilst the wretches dance backwards and forwards, making indecent gestures: the ropes rubbing their raw flesh all this time. Others, again, stick in their sides the pointed handles of iron shovels containing fire. Into this fire they every now and then throw Indian pitch, which for the moment blazes very high. Some monstrous shows (*gájan*) of paper vessels, elephants, and other fanciful and ridiculous pageants, are then exhibited and carried about, and, at noon, the crowds retire to their houses. The whole scene has a fiendish appearance, and the effect produced by these abominable and degrading superstitions is painful and sickening in the extreme.

On the evening of this day, the Sannyásis pierce the skin of their foreheads, and place a rod of iron in it as a socket; and on this rod fasten a lamp, which is kept burning nearly all the night, whilst the devotees are sitting opposite to or in Siva's temple, singing his praises, or calling upon him.

On the fourth day, in the afternoon, the *Charak* or swinging takes place. Iron hooks are fastened in the backs of the Sannyásis; after which they are suspended on a crossbeam placed on the top of a high post, which turns on a pivot, and is whirled round by means of ropes, with great rapidity. These swinging posts are generally erected in the most conspicuous places of the towns and villages, and often from 5 to 10 men swing, the one after the other, on one post. It is not very uncommon for the flesh of their back to tear, and then these poor deluded victims of superstition fall on the crowd below, and either are killed themselves, or kill those upon whom they fall. An awful instance of this happened at Chinsurah some years ago.

On this day, some Sannyásis cast themselves also from a bambu stage on iron spikes or knives stuck in bags of straw. These instruments, however, are generally laid in a reclining posture; so that when the person falls, they almost constantly are pressed down by his weight, and fall horizontally, instead of entering his body.

The deluded votaries of Siva inflict many other kinds of cruelties on themselves at this period: one only, as it is rather singular, will be mentioned. Some Sannyásis bedaub their lips with mud, and on this they scatter some mustard, or any other kind of small seed. They then lie down on their backs near Siva's temple, and do not move, nor eat, nor drink, until the seed has commenced germinating, which seldom happens before the third or fourth day.

On the following day, *viz.*, the 1st of *Báisak*, (the Hindu New-year's day,) some cooked rice, with broiled fish, is taken by a Bráhman, accompanied by the Sannyásis, to the place where the dead bodies are burnt, and there offered to departed spirits; after which, the Sannyásis shave, bathe and relinquish their *poitá*, and the festival is at an end.

**Changes in the Celebration.**—The foregoing account refers to former times. Hook swinging and falling upon knives are now forbidden. Wilkins says:

"At this season, too, there is a sort of carnival. Processions are formed and *tableaux vivants* arranged on platforms, representing different trades and professions, are carried through the streets. In former years the gestures as well as the scenes represented were of the most obscene character, but of late years these objectionable features have been largely curtailed."*

* *Modern Hinduism*, pp. 235, 236.

## HINDU NEW YEAR.

HINDU NEW YEAR.—The Hindu's astronomical year is sidereal. It is called *Samvatsaradi*—the first day of the year or the *Vishu-chantravishu*—the equinoctical point of Aries, into which the sun enters at the vernal equinox. This event generally falls on the 12th April and is considered by the Hindu a *punyakala*—holy occasion. So on New Year's Day the Manes and gods are propitiated by offerings of *tarpana*—oblations of water—and other allied ceremonies. In other respects, New Year's Day is a day of feasting.

Though thus the astronomical Hindu year falls on the 12th April, New Year's Day is observed on different days by different sects of Hindus, according as they happen to follow the lunar, the luni-solar or solar calendar. The Tamils follow the solar, and their year is thus the sidereal year. The Telugus and Canarese follow the *Chandramana* reckoning, and their year is luni-solar, which begins earlier than 12th April. The Malayalis follow the Tamils, though their *Koollam andu*—which is more an agricultural year—begins about the middle of September, when the sun enters the autumnal equinox.

On New Year's Day the elderly people—males and females—take a sacred bath in holy rivers or the sea, whichever happens to be nearest. The males propitiate the Manes and the deities; children appear in their holiday dress and jewels. The nearest temple is attended and the god in it is worshipped In some families children and other members receive new cloths. A sumptuous meal is cooked in every house, and poor relations are always cordially invited to the feast. At evening time the *Panchanga*, or the Calendar of the New Year, is read out and expounded by a holy Brahmin. Several people assemble to listen to this exposition. At the end of this ceremony, *attar*, *pansupari*, and dessert are distributed. Sometimes a short entertainment of music is also added to this ceremony. The whole day is spent more or less in mirth and festivity, and a light supper closes the day's proceedings.

In Malabar, the New Year's Day festivities are observed on a very grand scale. On New Year's eve all the gold coins available in the house, all gold jewels, all kinds of auspicious fruits and flowers and everything considered to be good to look at are placed in the room set apart for the worship of the family god. The Karnavan, who is the head of the family, first opens this room between 4 and 5 on New Year's morn and worships with a lighted lamp in his hand all these articles. Then every member of the house, one after the other, goes to the front of the room with his or her eyes shut and opens them when arrived at the proper spot to take a sight of the auspicious articles collected. The Karnavan—head of the family—presents each with something or other,—coins, jewels, flowers, fruits, etc. This is the chief difference between the Malayalis and other Hindus as regards the observance of New Year's festivities. And every Hindu takes care to see an auspicious sight on the New Year's morn, whether he is a Malayali or other Hindu.*

---

* *Madras Asylum Press Almanac.*

## HINDU JATRAS.

Wilkins gives the following general account of them:—

"As the Játras form an important part in most of the Hindu festivals, and as they are one of the most important agencies for teaching the people about Hinduism, a few words descriptive of them will not be inappropriate. These Játras come nearer to the old miracle plays of Europe than to anything else with which we are familiar. In front of the platform on which the image is placed is a space railed off for the performers. I have never seen them on a raised platform or stage; but as the front rows of people generally sit down, those standing behind can obtain a grand view of the performance. The actors are men and boys, who are in great request at these seasons. There is generally a band of music, which plays between the scenes of the Játra. The performance takes place immediately in front of the idol, although it can hardly be regarded as part of the worship, as it commences after the worship proper is over; yet it is supposed to be as much for the delight of the god as for the amusement of the people who gather to witness it. These plays which begin about eleven o'clock at night, and are continued until six or even seven o'clock the following morning, give representations of the important parts of the lives of the gods and goddesses of the Pantheon, the amours and amusements of Krishna, the quarrels of Siva and Párvatí, the life of Ráma and Sítá being the most common. The actors are dressed and painted in imitation of the deities they represent, and frequently their conversations are rendered attractive by sensual and obscene allusions; whilst in the interludes boys, dressed in women's clothes, dance with most indecent gestures. The worst dances that I have ever seen have been in front of an image, and as part of the rejoicings of a religious festival. Crowds of men, women, and children sit to watch them the whole night through, and certainly their theatrical representations of the acts and words of the deities form a most successful method of teaching the people the most memorable events of their lives. The words and dress of the actors being all according to the teaching of the Sástras, there can be no doubt that they exert an immense influence over the people. Lessons taught in this manner are not easily forgotten."*

## GOSTA JATRA.

*April.*

On this day, great crowds of *Vaishnavas*, and other Hindus assemble in some extensive field, erect a mound, and having placed on it the images of *Krishna* and *Rádhá*, worship them. Dramatic representations are exhibited, and much singing and feasting take place.

---

* *Modern Hinduism.* pp. 224, 225.

It may as well be remarked here, that the Hindus hold very early bathing during the whole month of *Baisák* (April-May) as exceedingly meritorious. Shástras say that those who do this acquire thereby as much religious merit as if they had presented the Bráhmans with a million of cows.

## Akhayi Tritia.

*About April 21st.*

This day is held sacred by the Hindus, because the Shástras declare that the merit of alms and gifts bestowed during it is permanent, and cannot be destroyed by any future sin; and therefore, even misers among them unloose their purse strings, and are liberal on that day. The women think that this day also is the most favorable of all for making *Kásundi*, which is a sort of pickle, prepared with unripe mangoes, tamarind, and mustard oil, and much liked by the natives.

## Savitri Brata.

*About April.*

*Sávitri* was the wife of king *Satyaván*, who lived in one of the former *Jugs*, and was a model of conjugal love and devotedness. The Hindu women, in imitation of her, on this day (1st of *Jaistha*), pay a kind of worship to their husbands, which they do by anointing them with powder of sandal-wood, adorning them with flowers, and presenting them with a new cloth. The performance of this ceremony, they believe, will ensure happiness and prosperity to their lords. On this occasion, *Yama* (the Hindu Pluto) is also worshipped by the women, who present him with offerings of rice, fruit, branches of the banyan tree, &c., with the intent that he may long spare the lives of their husbands.

## Aranya Sasthi.

This festival, which falls on the sixth day of the new moon in *Jaistha* (May-June) is celebrated only by women, in honour of the goddess *Sasthi*. The ceremonies on this occasion ought, according to the Shástras, to be performed in a forest; this is implied by the word *Aranya*. As such, however, are not everywhere near at hand, the pujá is made under any trees where the emblem of *Sasthi* is to be found. This emblem is a round black stone, painted red, and seen in most villages of Bengal. All the women of the place proceed thither with offerings of sweetmeats, plantains, &c., each having a fan in her hand, with which they refresh the stone-goddess, expecting that, moved by these acts of devotion, she will grant them fine, healthy children, or remove barrenness, should they be without offspring. The rule of the Shástras is, that roots only are to be used as food during the day; but this injunction is now laid aside, and bread and cakes are substituted.

## DASAHARA.

*About May 27th.*

This festival takes place on the tenth day of the increase of the moon of *Jaistha*. It is held in commemoration of the descent of *Gangá* to the earth. The Shástras say that this sacred river was originally only in heaven; but at the urgent prayer of the sage *Bhagirath*, the god *Brahmá* promised that it should flow on the earth also. As it had to fall from heaven to earth, *Bhagirath* was afraid lest the earth should be crushed by its fall: wherefore *Siva*, standing on mount *Himavat*, caught *Gangá* in his bunch of matted hair, and detained her there for some time; but at length suffered one drop to fall on the mountain, and from thence, on the 10th day after the new moon of *Jaistha*, the goddess touched the earth. Whichever way *Bhagirath* went, blowing the conch, thither *Gangá* it is said followed him.

Several very curious circumstances happened to *Ganga* as she passed along towards the sea. In one place she ran near *Jahnu*, a sage, and washed away his mendicant's dish, the flowers for worship, &c. Upon which he, in anger, took her up and swallowed her. At the entreaties of *Bhagirath*, however, the sage let her pass out at his ear, on which account Gangá received the name of *Jáhnavi!*

All Hindus keep the *Dasahará* festival. Crowds of people assemble from the different towns and villages near the river, especially at the most sacred places, as *Tribeni* and others, bringing their offerings of fruit, rice, cloth, sweetmeats, &c., which articles, after the worship of *Gangá* has been performed, are all appropriated by the officiating Bráhmans. The people often hang garlands of flowers across the river, even where it is very wide. Bloody sacrifices are also offered to the goddess, although at present very rarely.

The benefit accruing from worshipping *Gangá* on this day, is pardon of the following ten sins, viz. fornication, adultery, destruction of life, abusive language, falsehood, deceit, wanton words, covetousness, ill-will to others, and improper affections. When the star *Hastá Nakhyetra* is then on the meridian, the benefit is still greater, and extends to the pardon of the above-mentioned ten sins committed during ten previous births. And if this falls on a *Tuesday*, the merit of the worshipper is equal to that of having offered a million of times the sacrifice of a horse, and entitles him to become an *Indra* or King of Heaven.

## MANASA PUJA, NAG PANCHAMI.

During the year 1901 there perished from snake-bite in India 23,166 persons, the mortality in Bengal amounting to 11,130—nearly one-half. In the United Provinces, 5,110 deaths were reported; in Madras, 1902; Bombay, 1,160; Burma, 1,123; and Central Provinces, 1,804. It is not surprising, therefore, that snake worship prevails, especially in Bengal and the United Provinces.

**The Goddess worshipped.**—**Manasa** was sister of the serpent King Shesha, and wife of the sage Jarat-káru. She is represented as a handsome female of a golden colour, sitting on the water lily and clothed with snakes. She had special power in counteracting the venom of serpents, and was hence called *Visha-hará*, 'poison destroyer.'

**Snake worship in Bengal.**—Wilkins gives the following account of it:

"It occasions no surprise that in a country infested with snakes, some of which are so venomous that death follows their bite in half an hour, some protection from their baneful influence should be sought. And as they all, large and small, are supposed to be under the control of Manasá, she is worshipped with divine honours. A day or two before the festival it is no uncommon thing for mothers to prepare a dish of rice with treacle, which is placed before a pot of water under a village tree or in the house After it has been offered to the deity, it is eaten by the mother and her children, whom she hopes to preserve from these reptiles by this simple worship. At Manasá's festival, the snake charmers are called into requisition, and receive presents for their performance. These men, seated on a platform of bamboos, expose themselves to the bites of the most venomous reptiles, pretending that by their religious mantras they are proof against the poison. It may be that they are inoculated with it, or, what is more probable, the poison glands of these snakes have been previously removed. Some of these performers are remarkably skilful, for to hear them speak and watch their actions it would appear that there are snakes everywhere, that they have simply to call them and they appear. I have seen large snakes suddenly show themselves in most unexpected places where it has been indicated that it was the wish of the spectators that they should be found. The reason of this worship is found in stories in the Mahábhárata and elsewhere. It should be noticed that this, the chief worship of the snake deity, is held at the commencement of the rainy season, when, owing to the earth being saturated with moisture, snakes are driven from their holes, and become unusually destructive of human life."*

**Snake worship in North India.**—Crookes says:

"In the present day snake worship prevails widely. The great snake festival is as Nágapanchamí or 'dragon's fifth, "held on the

* *Modern Hinduism*, pp. 225, 226.

fifth day of the month Bhádon (August-September). In the Hills it is called the Rakhu or Barur Panchami. Rakhesvar has now become a title of Siva as lord of the Nágas, a form in which he is represented as surrounded by serpents and crowned with a chaplet of hooded snakes. On the day of the feast the people paint figures of serpents and birds on the walls of their houses, and seven days before the festival they steep a mixture of wheat, gram, and pulse in water. On the morning of the feast they take a wisp of grass, tie it up in the form of a snake, dip it in the water in which the grain has been steeped, and offer it with money and sweetmeats to the serpents. In Udaypur on this day they strew particular plants about the threshold of houses to prevent the entrance of venomous reptiles, and in Nepál, the day is observed as the anniversary of a great struggle between a famous Nág and Garuda, the foe of the serpent race. In the eastern districts of the North-Western Provinces on this day milk and dried rice are poured into a snake's hole; while doing this they merely call out 'Snake! Snake!' and in Behar low caste women go about singing songs to propitiate snakes. In Bombay during the feast snakes are fed in a curious way described by Mr. Rousselet. After the Diwáli in Kangra a festival is held to say good-bye to snakes, at which an image of the Nág made of cow-dung is worshipped. If a snake is seen soon after that, it is called 'ungrateful,' and immediately killed.

"In the North-Western Provinces the usual custom is for the head of the family to bathe on the morning of the feast, to paint on the wall of his sleeping room two rude representations of serpents, and to make offerings to Brahmans. The women also make a snake-like line of flour all round the dwelling-house as a sort of magic circle through which no snake can pass. On this day many people pray to what Dr. Buchanan calls 'the chief eight dragons of the pot'; girls throw some playthings into the water; labourers take a holiday, and worship the tools of their craft. In Behár during the month of Sáwan (August) crowds of women, calling themselves Nágin or wives of the snake, go about begging for $2\frac{1}{2}$ days, during which they neither sleep under a roof nor eat salt. Half the proceeds of the begging is given to Brahmans and the other half invested in salt and sweetmeats, which are eaten by all the people of the village. In Garhwál the ground is freely smeared with cow-dung and mud, and figures of 5, 7, or 9 serpents are rudely drawn with sandal wood powder or turmeric; rice, beans, or gram are parched; lamps are lighted and waved before them, incense is burnt, and food and fruit offered. These observances take place both morning and evening, and the night is spent in listening to stories in praise of the Nág."*

## SNAN (BATHING) JATRA.

*About June 2nd.*

Puri (the city) in Orissa is the chief seat of the worship of Jagannath, but it is also popular in Bengal. There are three festivals connected with his worship. The first, called *Snán*

* *Popular Religion of Northern India*, pp. 272, 273.

*Jatra,* is observed on the full moon of Jaishta, (May-June) the second month of the Hindu year.

Wilkins gives the following account of its observance in Bengal:

"At some places in Calcutta this ceremony is performed. Near Serampore, in a village, called Mahesh, is a temple with cars almost as ponderous as those at Puri, that are called into requisition in the following month for the Rath Jatra which attracts almost as many people from the neighbourhood as Puri itself, while most large village has its own car for the festival. The ceremonies are much the same as those at Puri; but, being performed in a place which has no sacred enclosure to shut out the non-Hindu population, it can be witnessed by any who wish to do so. And I certainly think that, of all the festivals of Hindus, this is the most imposing that I have seen. On this occasion the image that has been kept in its shrine since the similar festival of the preceding year is brought outside the temple, and on a high platform erected for the occasion, bathed, anointed with holy oil and clothed by the priests, in the sight of an immense concourse of the people. From 60,000 to 80,000 people stand round this platform with their gaze directed to the priests engaged in their holy work, and as the time for its completion approaches, there is scarcely a sound heard. Many of the people probably have gone there out of mere curiosity, some have gone simply for amusement; but multitudes, it is certain, have been brought there by the earnest desire to see Jagannátha, the sight of whom they believe will take away all their sins.

"At length the bath and the robing being completed, the god is raised up so that the people can see him; and from the vast crowd there goes forth a shout, 'Jai Jai Jagannátha! Jai Jai Jagannátha!' * which once heard will never be forgotten. On this occasion the whole neighbourhood has the appearance of a fair, and when the religious ceremony is over, the fair begins. There are stalls with all kinds of goods for sale, shows, and various kinds of amusement. And as the great majority of fallen women, having been outcasted when they took to a life of immorality, have become Vaishnavas, they are to be found in great numbers at this, almost the only religious festival in which they can have a share. Certainly the music, dancing, and general merry-making, that prevail after the religious feast of the festival is over, are altogether out of harmony with what has always appeared to me as the most impressive ceremony I have seen connected with Hinduism. Every large town and many villages have their image of Jagannátha, so that yearly there is the observance of this festival within an easy distance of almost every part of Bengal. It is my belief that this festival is more largely attended and its lessons more widely taught than those perhaps of any other, not excepting even the Durgá Puja. There are ceremonies, such as the sacrificing of goats in the Durgá Puja, that offend the prejudices of the more earnest followers of Vishnu; but in Jagannátha's worship, as it is practised

---

* Victory to Jagannáth, i.

away from Puri, there is nothing to offend the prejudices of any Hindu. At Puri caste distinctions are ignored; but this is not common at other places."*

All those who go to see this ceremony are assured in the Shástras, that they shall be subject to no more births; but be admitted into the heaven of *Vishnu*, after the death of this body.

### GOSAHASRI.

This is a bathing festival, and takes place on the new moon of *Asharh* (June-July). The merit of bathing in the Ganges this day is equal to that of bestowing a gift of a thousand cows on the Bráhmans, and entitles the performer to a residence in heaven of as many years as there are hairs on the bodies of that number of kine.

### AMBU BASI.

This and the two following days the goddess *Prithivi*, or the Earth, is, according to the Shástras, subject to her periodical uncleanness. The Hindus are strictly prohibited during these three days to dig the earth, to sow any kind of seed, and to commence any new undertaking.

Crooke says:

"Throughout Northern India the belief in the sanctity of earth is universal. The dying man is laid on the earth, and so is the mother at the time of parturition.

"There are certain days on which ploughing is unlawful, the N. g-panchami or snake feast held on the 5th of the light half of Sáwa and the 15th of the month Kártik. But Mother Earth is supposed to sleep on six days in every month—the 5th, 7th, 9th, 11th, 21st and 24th, or, as others say—the 1st, 2nd, 5th, 7th, 10th, 21st and 24th. On such days it is advisable not to plough if it can possibly be avoided. The 15 days in the month of Kuár, which are devoted to the worship of the Pitris or sainted dead, are also an inauspicious time for agricultural work."†

### RATH (CAR) JATRA.

*About July 17th.*

For 15 days after the Snan Játra Jagannátha remains invisible to the public. It is supposed that by his exposure on that occasion he caught cold, and suffers from fever during the days he remains invisible. At Puri, this is the time for cleaning and repainting the image which, owing to the many offerings of the worshippers and oil lamps burning day and night, has become covered with dirt.

---

* *Modern Hinduism*, pp. 220, 221.

† *Popular Religion, &c., of Northern India*, pp. 15, 372.

The god having recovered from his indisposition at the Rath Játra, is taken out of his temple with his brother Balaráma and his sister Subhadrá, and ropes having been fixed to them they are drawn up and seated on benches in an elevated part of the *Rath*, which is an immense car in the shape of a tapering tower, sometimes 30 to 40 cubits high. Hawsers of great length and thickness having been fastened to the ponderous machine, hundreds and often thousands of people take hold of the same, and draw it amidst most deafening shouts. When arrived at a certain fixed spot, the priests take down the images, and carry them to the temple of some other god, where they remain eight days. They are then said to be paying a visit to that god. The car, with its disgusting and demoralizing exhibitions, during that period remains exposed to public view.

Wilkins says, " In former days, these cars were, and in some out of the way places are still, adorned with most obscene pictures; but the purer tastes of the people or the watchful eyes of the magistrates being averse to this, in most places they have disappeared." It is to be feared that the reform is not at all general.

## ULTA RATH.

*July 25th.*

The following account is from Wilkins :

"The Ulta Rath is the return of Jagannátha to his temple. About a fortnight after the Car Festival, another of a somewhat similar character is held, though it is by no means so popular as the former. The image of Jagannátha is brought out from the temple where it has been on a visit, placed upon the car, and then dragged back to its own proper temple. The people come in large numbers, but there is nothing like the same enthusiasm manifested as when the deity was taken out for his visit. Sometimes the people have to be rewarded by sweetmeats, &c., to induce them to give assistance in dragging the car; whilst at the Car Festival there were more volunteers than necessary.

"To assist in the holy work of removing the ponderous car is believed by the more superstitious to secure the favour of the god, and to improve their position in heaven. Jagannátha being a form of Vishnu, it is this great deity's favour that is obtained when honour is shown to the idol; hence the Vaishnavas, as a whole, take part in these ceremonies.*

## SAYAN EKADASI.

This is held on the 11th of the light half of the month Asharh, the fourth month of the Hindu solar year (June-July). It is the summer solstice and considered in Bengal the first of

* *Modern Hinduism*, pp. 223, 224.

the rainy season. Vishnu is then fabled to go to sleep for four months on the serpent Shesha. A very strict fast should be observed on the occasion.

### Manwantara.

A *Manwantara* is the period of the existence of a Manu, 4,320,000 years.

This is the anniversary of a new *Manu* taking the government of the world. It is a bathing festival, and those who on this day perform their ablutions in the Ganges are assured that the merit of their good actions, and especially of their deeds of charity, will never be obliterated by any future sins.

### Jhulan (Swinging) Jatra.

*August 25th.*

From the new until the full moon of August, the *Jhulan Jatra* is celebrated, to commemorate the frolics of Krishna and Rádhá. Many Hindus keep this feast only for five nights, beginning on the eleventh day of the moon; and others for three nights, commencing on the thirteenth.

The ceremonies gone through are much the same as those of the *Dola Jatra*, described above; only that no *phag* (red powder) is used as on that occasion, and that the god and his mistress have daily a new change of raiment given them as long as the festival lasts. Krishna and Rádhá are placed in a chair suspended from the ceiling, and swung first by the proprietor of the house, and afterwards by the Brahman guests at pleasure. About 10 o'clock the images are worshipped in the usual way, and offerings of fruits, sweetmeats, cloth, &c., presented. At this time a great number of persons attend outside, and make a horrid discord with barbarous instruments of music, connecting the whole with every kind of indecency.

At noon, the person at whose house the festival is held, generally gives a grand entertainment to Brahmans and others. After eating, dances and dramatic exhibitions of the most indelicate and obscene kind take place, and love-songs in honour of Krishna and Rádhá are sung. The festivities are thus continued till the crowd retire at day-light.

### Cocoa-nut Day, Narali Purnami.

On the full moon of Shravan (July-August) the stormy part of the south-west monsoon is considered to be at an end in Bombay, and cocoa-nuts are offered to the sea to gain its favour towards those who now begin to trust themselves to its mercy.

## RAKSHA CANDHAN.

*About August 29th.*

This is a recognised festival in the United Provinces. It is held on the full moon of Sáwan. Knotted cords are tied by women round the wrists of their friends as a protection against demons. Crooke says:

"Connected with this is what is known as the Barley Feast (*Jayi* or *Jawára*) in Upper India and Bhujaríya-in the Central Provinces. All that is usually due is that on the 7th day of the light half of Sáwan, grains of barley are sown in a pot of manure, and spring up so rapidly, that by the end of the month the vessel is full of long yellowish, green stalks. On the first day of the next month Bhádon, women and girls take them out, throw the earth and manure into water, and distribute the plants to their male friends who bind them in their turban and about their dress. It is emblematical of the healthy growth of the seedlings at the approaching sowing of the winter crops."*

## JANMA (BIRTH) ASHTAMNI.

*About August 5th.*

This is the anniversary of Krishna's birth-day. On the first day Hindus fast and repair to temples where images of this god are bathed with *panchámirt*, a mixture of milk, curdled milk, ghee, sugar, and honey, and worshipped with incense, flowers, &c. People partake of holy offerings, and at nights sing hymns in praise of the god. The next day they again repair to temples, singing and sounding cymbals and playing on various other sorts of musical instruments, and show their rejoicing for the god's birth by throwing on each other curdled milk coloured with powdered turmeric; this is called Dad kándo.†

## NANDOTSAB.

On this day, *Nanda*, the reputed father of *Krishna,* had public rejoicing on account of the birth of his son; in commemoration of which the Hindus keep up a kind of a carnival, throwing turmeric water at each other, singing licentious songs, and performing dramatic exhibitions, all relating to the history of *Krishna*, and very demoralizing in their tendency.

---

* *Popular Religion of Northern India*, pp. 373, 374.

† *Manners and Customs of Hindus of Northern India*, by Ishuree Dass, pp. 110, 111.

## Ganesh or Vinayaka Chaturthi.

*End of August.*

Ganesa, said to be the son of Siva and Párvatí or of Párvatí alone, is worshipped under the names of Ganesa, Vinayaka, Ganapati, Pillayar, &c. He is worshipped in every Hindu home. Every school boy begins his lessons by lessons with Sri Ganesáya namah; every Indian book opens with it. Every merchant asks his help before commencing any business. In marriages and every kind of religious ceremonies, Vinayaka is first invoked.

By some Ganesa is described as the god of learning, but that is the province of Sarasvatí. A Hindu thinks that if his literary efforts are a failure, this is not due to his own incapacity, but to demoniacal obstruction. The aid of Ganesa, as lord of demons, is therefore sought.

*Chaturthi* means fourth. This festival is celebrated on the fourth lunar day of the bright half of the month Simha. In South India rice puddings are offered to the god, to be afterwards consumed by the family. A fresh image of Ganesa in clay is made and worshipped. The 108 names of the god are repeated, and flowers are offered to him.

**Looking at the moon forbidden on Ganesh Chaturthi.**—A legend thus accounts for the origin of this prohibition:

One day Ganapati, while riding on his favourite rat, had a fall, at which the moon laughed Enraged at such an insult, the god of prudence cursed the moon and all who should look at her; but afterwards amended the matter by restricting any from looking at her on his birthday. Thus, on the day of Ganesh Chaturthi the Hindus are prohibited by the Shástras from looking at the moon, and are afraid to look at it this evening lest they should incur any calamity during the year; and if by any accident they happen to see it, they try to provoke their neighbours to revile them, and comfort themselves with the idea that the calamities incurred will be all comprehended in the abuse, and removed by it.*

## Mahalaya Amavasa.

*September.*

*Amavasa* denotes the day of the conjunction of the sun and moon occurring once a month. By Hindus it is specially set apart for offerings and the performance of religious ceremonies to the *Pitris;* or the spirits of departed ancestors. It is said that when the sun enters the sign *Virgo*, the Pitris, leaving the world of Yama, come down to the world of man, and occupy the houses of their descendants in this world. The fortnight preceding the new

* *Bombay Almanack.*

moon of the month *Virgo* is considered sacred to the propitiation of the Pitris. The ceremonies during each day of this fortnight are considered to be equal to the ceremonies performed at Gaya. The ceremonies terminate on the Mahalaya Amavasa day, which is therefore observed with greater sanctity.

## ANANTA BRATA.

On this day sweetmeats and all kinds of fruits are offered to *Krishna;* and every one who does it for fourteen years consecutively, is promised the highest bliss in *Vishnu's* heaven.

## RAM LILA.

This is a dramatic representation, very popular in North India, of the victory of Ráma over Rávana and the recovery of Sitá. An enclosure is made of bamboos, covered with paper and painted to represent a fortress. Within it is a frightful paper giant, fifteen feet high with ten or twelve arms, each grasping either a sword, a bow, a battle-axe or a spear. At his feet is Sitá, sitting disconsolate, guarded by two figures to represent demons. Hanumán is represented naked and hairy, with a long tail tied round his waist, a mask to represent the head of a baboon, and two great painted clubs in his hands. His army follows, a number of men with similar tails and masks, their bodies dyed with indigo, and also armed with clubs. After Rávana is slain by Ráma, the images of Rávana and the other giants with their fortress, are set on fire and consumed. The festival concludes with Sitá's release, purification, and remarriage to Ráma.

## DURGA PUJA.

*October.*

This is the most popular festival in Bengal. The following account of it is from Wilkins:

"A Hindu who determines to have the Durgá Pujá celebrated in his house, on the day of the Rath Játra takes a piece* of split bamboo into the room where the family idols are kept, and the family priest, after a prayer to Vishnu, anoints it with sandalwood paste, and invokes Durgá's blessing upon it. This bamboo remains there until the Janma Ashtami, *i.e.*, the birth-day of Krishna, when the maker of the image removes it, that the work of constructing the idol may commence. The materials for this purpose—bamboos, grass, and Ganges mud, are carefully selected, and on an auspicious moment the holes are drilled in a piece of wood on which the images are to be fixed. When this is done, and the rough sketches made, they are covered with a preparation of mud, cow-dung, and the husks of rice. The figures that cluster

---

* Abridged from *Hindu Feasts, Fasts, and Ceremonies.*

around Durgá are her two sons Kárttikeya and Ganesa; and Sarasvatí, the bride of Brahmá, and Lakshmí the wife of Vishnu. There are also representations of Mahesha, the buffalo-headed Asura whom Durgá came to slay. When the figures are dry, at appointed times the painters come to paint and the decorators to adorn the image. Round these figures, on what is called a roof, but which is really a circle, divided into compartments, pictures of other deities are painted, or some mythological scenes represented. These vary considerably according to the taste of the gentleman in whose house and at whose expense the worship is carried on. The central figure, Durgá, has ten hands, in which are various weapons; for though bearing a most mild and gentle expression, it is supposed to represent her when victorious over the great Asura, the enemy of gods and men.

"The worship may be performed or not, according to the religious state of the householder. On the one hand, it is a sin of omission to neglect it, whilst to perform it will cause great good to the worshipper. One Sastra says. 'Whoever from ignorance, vanity, or jealousy, or from any other cause, does not worship Deví (Durgá) the wrath of the goddess falls on him, and destroys all his wishes.' Another declares that 'the gratification of Bhavání is the assurance of happiness for the whole year, is for the destruction of spirits, goblins and ghosts, and for the sake of festivity.' Another appeals still more strongly, as it declares that 'the meritorious effects of gratifying Durgá, even for half a minute, cannot be described by Mahesh (Siva), the five-faced, in a hundred years.' When circumstances prevent a man from incurring the expense of setting up an image in his own house, it is no uncommon thing to worship her as represented by a picture or a jar of water, or to send their offerings to the temporary shrine that is set up at the house of a neighbour or relative. It is declared in one of the Puránas that the offerings of even slaves and outcasts are acceptable to the goddess at these festive occasions.

"The first part of the ceremony is the *Bodhána*, or the awaking of the goddess, who is supposed to have been sleeping for the past two months, a part of which ceremony is the worshipping of a twig of the bél-tree, which is especially dear to her. The texts differ as to when this ceremony should take place. When the time arrives for the commencement of the worship, the head of the family, after certain purifying ceremonies, declares his name and expresses his purpose to perform the Durgá Puja with proper rites. He then, in due form, appoints the officiating priests, who in his name and on his behalf perform the ceremonies. The priests then go through a long and tedious list of ceremonies, worshipping other deities as well as Durgá, and sanctifying by their mantras all the various implements, &c., that are used in the celebration. Part of the worship is called Dhyán or meditation, in which the priest thinks of Durgá according to the representation that is then before him. The most interesting part of the ceremony is that in which the goddess is invited to visit the house, and dwell in the image prepared for her. The priest, in order to obtain this blessing, after several other ceremonies have been performed, places his right hand on the breast of the image and says, 'Om!'

welcome, Deví, to my house with thy eight Saktas. O Dispenser of blessings: O Lotus-eyed, I perform this autumnal festival. Respond to me O great goddess...Annihilator of all transgressions in this unfordable ocean of the world. Save me, blessed goddess, I salute thee, beloved. O Sankara (Siva) protect my life, my honour, my offspring, my wives, and my wealth. As thou art the only defender of all, O goddess, the most beloved in the world, enter and stay with this sacrifice as long as I am worshipping thee." First the right eye, then the left, then the eye on the forehead are touched by the priest, and after that the other parts of the body, and an appropriate mantra recited, by which means the ceremony of *Prânpratishta*, or the giving of life to the image, is performed. After this all the various vessels and articles used in the worship are sanctified by mantras.

"For three mornings and three evenings the worship is continued In some houses, though not in all, a kid, or three, or seven are sacrificed. In some cases a buffalo is added. The victim is sanctified by certain ceremonies, Ganges water is sprinkled on its head, a little vermilion is placed on its forehead, and its head having been made fast in a strong frame, with one blow of the sacrificial knife is severed from the body. A little of the blood and a piece of flesh is then placed before the image.

"On the afternoon of the fourth day the goddess is supposed to take leave of the image. Most elaborate dismissal ceremonies are gone through, and an invitation is given to her to return at the next annual festival. When this is over the image is taken down from the platform, and the women of the household walk round it, and throw rice, water, and betel leaves upon it. It is then carried to the river-side, and accompanied by music, cast into the stream amid the shouts of the spectators.

"This festival in Bengal is the most popular of all. It is a universal holiday, and at this season husbands and sons, who by their business may have been absent from their homes, endeavour to rejoin their families. It is not inaptly termed the Christmas of Bengal, in the sense that it is a time of universal rejoicing and merriment In front of the image at this festival, as at others already described, there is the usual singing, dancing, and theatrical representation throughout the whole night. As these images are set up in the villages as well as in the towns, the poorer people are able to attend them. And when it is remembered that the amusements are perfectly free for all, it is not surprising that immense crowds are seen at these religious festivals. In the three nights of the Puja, Calcutta is awake the whole night, and any one unacquainted with the cause, as the drums are beating all over the city, might fancy that the whole city was in arms. And although these nights are given to merriment, the police have little to do except to keep the vehicles in motion, in order to prevent a block. Occasionally a few drunken men are seen, but this is a rare exception. As a rule, the immense crowds that are afoot are most peaceably inclined, and well conducted as they walk from house to house to see the játras and nautches."*

* *Modern Hinduism*, pp. 227, 231.

The following remarks on the Durgá Puja are abridged from the *Indian Messenger* :—

"It has features which at once command our sympathy. The resources of the poorest are now taxed to make little love-offerings to those to whom they are bound by social ties. Brothers hasten home from their distant places of business, once more lighting up with their countenances the long-deserted homes. But alas! there are other features as well which produce quite another impression upon the mind. This wave of national sentiment also covers an amount of self-indulgence and excess, which is quite appalling. This is also the period for all the votaries of pleasure to run headlong into their vicious excesses. Drunkenness and debauchery will ride rampant in the land for many days." Sept. 25th, 1887.

There are not now the grand entertainments at the Durgá Puja as in former times. One of the chief features at present is the stock of wines and spirits provided by shopkeepers.

### Lakshmi Puja.

*About October 27th.*

This festival, in honour of Lakshmí, wife of Vishnu, and goddess of prosperity, takes place on the night of the full moon following the Durgá Puja. The worship is generally performed before a corn basket painted red, filled with rice, decorated with flowers and covered with a piece of cloth. Sometimes, however, an image is made in the shape of a handsome female sitting on the water-lily holding a necklace in her left hand, and spreading out the right to bestow her blessing. The Hindus are very particular in worshipping *Lakshmí*, scarcely ever omitting to pay her due homage; and her favour, as being the giver of *temporal* prosperity, is sought more eagerly by them than that of such gods or goddesses as reward their votaries only in the next world.

As Lakshmí is supposed during the night to pass over all who may be awake, it is usual for the people to sit up playing cards or amusing themselves in some way, so as to keep themselves awake.

### Dipavali.

*About October 20th.*

Dipavali (*Dipa*, a lamp, and *Avali*, a row), "the feasts of lamps, is a festival on the new moon of *Kártik*, celebrated in honour of the goddess Kalí, or Bhawaní, who was formerly propitiated by human sacrifices, and of Vishnu's victory over the demon Naraka. The festival, however, seems to be more peculiarly consecrated to Lakshmí, or the goddess of prosperity. The feast begins on the 13th day of Ashwin Vad, termed Dhanatrayodashi (from *Dhan*, wealth; *Trayodashi*, 13th), and money-lenders now count their stores and perform puja to their wealth. It is celebrated for a period of five days, during which houses are cleaned, whitewashed, and illuminated; a quadrangular floor, called Ranguli, is made in front of the house and painted with different coloured powders. Gambling is vigorously carried on, and is the chief recreation of the feast. All the treasure in the house is collected and worshipped under the name of Lakshmi, the goddess of wealth; a light is made and dedicated to Yama, the god of the infernal regions: and every preparation made for the succeeding morning. Fireworks, crackers, spouters, &c., are displayed. The 14th is Narak Chaturdashi (*Narak; Chaturdashi*, 14th), on which Vishnu is fabled to have killed Narakasura, a giant, and entered his city early in the morning, when the people illuminated the city and received him with great joy and acclamation; and the women, having adorned themselves, went before him with lighted lamps. The Hindus keep this day to commemorate this great conquest. They get up early in the morning, fill the house with lights, rub their bodies with perfumed ointment, and bathe themselves with hot water. No member of the family is left unbathed, new clothes and ornaments are put on, and the children are decorated. This done, the mistress of the house performs a sort of ceremony called *Arti*, placing wicks either in silver or brass dishes, symbolical of the removal of all their difficulties, and of a happy year, when each male member makes her a present of money. Sweetmeats are distributed and friends are invited to dinner. The 30th Amavasya, or the last day of the moon, is the day of Sarasvatí, the goddess of learning, the same as Lakshmí, the goddess of wealth. It is known by the name of Vahipulan, or the worship of the shop records. This day the Vikramaditya Samvat year ends. All the merchants close their accounts this evening. New journals, ledgers, and day-books are brought and worshipped through a Brahmin priest; new entries are made in the account-books; writers are sent to different shops with money to credit in their names on this auspicious evening; Sarasvatí is invoked to render the following year prosperous, and to be with them throughout it; then the Brahmins are sufficiently paid for their labours, and the servants receive a present of money according to their rank.*

## KRITTIKA.

*About December 3rd.*

This is a South Indian festival, somewhat like the Dipavali. It is in honour of Siva's appearance as a fire pillar, the top and bottom of which Brahmá and Vishnu could not discover. Near Siva temples a rod, 25 or 30 feet high, is planted and covered with dried palm leaves. In the evening when the idol of Siva is taken out in procession, a halt is made before the pillar, lighted camphor is thrown upon it, and it blazes up. A row of lights is

* *Madras Almanack.*

placed in front of every house, and children fire crackers. Where temples stand on hills, the whole rock is illuminated.

The large amount spent on crackers is one of the causes of India's poverty. Every year also they lead to accidents.

### Kali or Shyama Puja.

*About November 10th.*

This festival is celebrated at the new moon in honour of the goddess *Kalí*, who is a form of *Durgá*.

The image of *Kali* is that of a very black female, with four arms, having in one hand a scymitar and in another the head of a giant which she holds by the hair; another hand is spread open as bestowing a blessing, and with the fourth she is forbidding fear. She wears two dead bodies for earrings, and a necklace of skulls; and her tongue hangs down to her chin. The hands of several giants are hung as a girdle round her loins, and her dishevelled hair falls down to her heels. She stands on the body of her husband *Siva*, who is represented as a white man extended at full length upon his back.

The reason of this singular posture of the goddess is thus related. *Kalí* having destroyed the giants *Raktabij*, *Shumbha*, *Nishumbha*, and their adherents, who had placed the gods in great jeopardy, was so overjoyed at her victory, that she danced till the earth shook to its foundation, and *Siva*, at the intercession of the gods, was compelled to go to the spot to persuade her to desist. He, however, found her so elated that he despaired of making any impression on her by words, and therefore adopted another expedient: he threw himself among the dead bodies of the slain, and when the goddess looking down perceived that she was dancing on her husband, was so shocked, that to express her surprise, she put out her tongue to a great length and remained motionless, and thus the earth was saved from the imminent danger to which it was exposed.

The worship takes place at night, and is always accompanied with bloody sacrifices. Many of the worshippers afterwards partake of flesh and spirituous liquors;—of the latter, generally to such an immoderate degree, as to produce shameful intoxication; and all this under the name of religion! On the following day the image is cast into the river with the same ceremonies as are used with the image of *Durgá*.

There are in Bengal, besides the clay images of *Kalí* which are made annually, many permanent ones, generally of stone, which are worshipped all the year round. The principal one of these is at a village three miles south of Calcutta, and on this account called *Kalí Ghat*.

## BHRATRIDWITIYA.

*About November 13th.*

On this day, sisters make it a point to adorn their brothers by making a mark on their foreheads with powder of sandal wood; after which they feast them with every kind of delicacy, and, when they can afford it, make them presents of cloth. They imagine that by this means the lives of their brothers will be lengthened, and *Yama*, the regent of *death*, will have no power over them; as is expressed in the two following lines, which they repeat on that occasion—

> On my brother's brow I have made the mark,
> On Yama's door the bolt has fallen.

## KARTTIK PUJA (TWO DAYS).

*About November 13th.*

KARTTIKEYA, also called SKANDA and in the south SUBRAMANYA, was the god of war. Different accounts are given of his origin. He is usually said to be the son of Siva without the intervention of a woman. He was born for the purpose of destroying Táraka, a Daitya whose austerities had made him formidable to the gods. He is represented as riding on a peacock, with a bow in one hand and an arrow in the other.

A clay image of this god is worshipped on the first day at night, once at every watch; and on the following day it is thrown into the river. No bloody sacrifices are offered. Married persons desirous of offspring are among the principal worshippers of *Kárttikeya*, whose power is believed to be unlimited in conferring that boon. The beauty of *Kárttikeya* is quite proverbial among the Hindus.

## JAGADDHATRI PUJA.

*About November 20th.*

*Jagaddhatri*, the nurse or mother of the world, is another form of *Durgá*; she is represented as a *yellow* woman, dressed in red, and sitting on a lion. At this time a very popular festival is held in her honour, when bloody sacrifices are offered, and large sums expended in illuminations, dances, songs, feasting the Brahmans, &c. Much indecent mirth takes place, and numbers of men dance naked before the image, deeming that highly meritorious and pleasing to the deity. The benefits expected from this worship are the four things usually promised in the Hindu Shastras by the gods to their votaries; *viz.*, the fruit of meritorious actions—riches—the gratification of every desire—and future happiness.

## RAS LILA OR RAS JATRA.

*About November 25th.*

The following account of the origin of this festival is abridged from the Vishnu Purána:

"Krishna observing the clear sky bright with the autumnal moon, felt inclined to join with the Gopís in sport. Accordingly he commenced singing sweet strains such as the women loved; so they, as soon as they heard the melody, quitted their homes, and hastened to meet Krishna. Then Madhava,* coming amongst them, conciliated some with soft speeches, some with gentle looks, and some he took by the hand; and the illustrious deity sported with them in the stations of the dance. Then proceeded the dance to the music of their clashing bracelets. At times, one of the nymphs, wearied by the revolving dance, threw her arms, ornamented with tinkling bracelets, round the neck of the destroyer of Madha; another skilled in the art of singing his praises, embraced him. When leading, they followed him; when returning they encountered him; and, whether he went forwards or backwards they ever attended on his steps. Whilst frolicking thus with the Gopís, they considered every instant without him a myriad of years; and, prohibited in vain by husbands, fathers, brothers, they went forth at night to sport with Krishna, the object of their affection.†

In North India men and women holding each other's hands, go round in a circle, singing the airs to which they dance, in imitation of Krishna and the Gopís.

The following account is given of its celebration in Bengal under the name of Ras Játra:

This festival is held during three nights, to celebrate the revels of *Krishna* with the milkmaids. The image of this god is placed in a brick building, which is open on all sides, and has one highly elevated sitting-place. This building is annually ornamented and grandly illuminated for the festival. Sixteen small images of *Krishna* are necessary on this occasion; but a very small gold image, about the size of a breast-pin, is placed as the object of adoration, and afterwards given to the officiating Brahman. At the close of the festival the clay images are thrown into the river.

Round the building in the street, booths are erected, filled with sweetmeats, playthings, and other articles, like a European fair. Numbers of persons of all ages visit the spot; and as usual at all festivals kept in honour of this impure god, most licentious songs are sung and indecent dances take place.

---

* A name of Krishna is the slayer of the demon Madha.

† *Vishnu Purána*, Book V., Chapter 13.

Wilkins says, "This is a most popular festival, and immense crowds of people come to this annual fair with all the attendant festivities and excesses."

### SURJYA PUJA, OR ITA PUJA.

*November.*

On the last day of the month of *Kártik,* the last of *Aghran* and every intervening Sunday, the worship of *Surjya* or the Sun is performed. The Hindu Apollo is represented as a dark-red man, with three eyes and four arms; in two hands he holds the water-lily, with another he is bestowing a blessing, and with the other forbidding fear. He sits on a red water-lily, and rays of glory issue from his body.

On the present occasion, no image of this god is made; but a small earthen pot painted red, on the top of which two betel leaves and a plantain leaf are placed, is used as the object of worship. The offerings consist of red flowers, dub-grass, rice boiled in milk (*paramanna*) and rice-cakes (*pishtak*). Food of this soft description is presented to *Surjya,* owing to his being destitute of the organs of mastication, he having had all his teeth knocked out of his mouth by the giant *Bir Bhadra* at the celebrated festival of the gods given by *Daksha* the son of *Brahma!*

The principal benefit expected from this worship, is preservation from disease; it being the special department of *Surjya* to confer health, as it is that of *Kártik* to give offspring,—that of *Ganesa* to remove difficulties,—that of *Durgá* to satisfy all desires,—that of *Siva* to impart knowledge, and that of *Vishnu* to bestow 'salvation.'

The persons who receive the name of *Surjya,* and adopt this god as their guardian deity, are called *Sauras:* they never eat till they have worshipped the Sun, and when the Sun is entirely covered with clouds, they fast. On a Sunday, which is particularly consecrated to the Sun, the *Sauras,* as well as Hindus belonging to other sects, perform, in a more particular manner, the worship of this idol, and some of them fast, at least partially: abstaining from all animal food, whether it be fish or flesh.

### FESTIVAL OF FIRST FRUITS.

*November-December.*

It is thus described by Wilkins:

"This festival is held at the season when the new rice is ripe. An offering of rice, milk, and fruits, is first made to the gods, then to the great progenitors of mankind, then to the cattle, then to the scavengers, *i.e.*, crows and jackals, and then the people partake of some themselves."*

---

* *Modern Hinduism,* pp. 233, 234.

## RURAL FESTIVALS.

A number of these are described by Crooke, connected with ploughing, cattle, ceremonies to avert blight, locusts, &c., betel planting, cotton planting, winnowing, &c.*

### THE ONAM FESTIVAL IN MALABAR.

*August-September.*

The legend on which the obligation of this festival is made to rest, is to the effect that a great king, Mahábali, by his religious austerities had obtained such extraordinary merit and authority as to alarm the gods themselves, and cause them to tremble for their supremacy. Vishnu, thereupon, taking the form of a dwarf† asked of the king as much land as he could measure out by three steps. The request was granted. Immediately expanding to a gigantic size, the god took one step half round the world, another step completed the circuit, and the third was taken by placing his foot on the head of the unfortunate king and crushing him down to the infernal regions, where, however, he was permitted to exercise sovereignty. Once a year on this night, he returns to earth, and wanders about to see if his people are thriving. They endeavour, therefore, to appear as joyful and happy as possible.

The Onam, celebrated in August or September, is the great national festival in Malabar. Everything is now green and fresh after the rains, so that this almost amounts to a spring feast. Houses are decorated with flowers, lamps are kept burning, new clothes and earthenware purchased and the old thrown away, swings are in general requisition, and a jubilee is kept by all ranks and conditions of the people.‡

After the feast is over, there is a grand sham fight.

### REMARKS ON HINDU FESTIVALS.

The principal festivals were founded on the changes of the seasons; as spring, autumn, the time when the sun begins its course to the south, &c. Nearly all have foolish legends connected with them, in honour of the gods and goddesses worshipped. The Durgá puja celebrates an imaginary fight, and worship is paid to her instead of the one true God, the source of all our blessings.

Bishop Caldwell thus describes the festivals of the Hindus:

"The 'divine worship' which they perform on these festival nights, consists merely in drumming and shouting, in flags and guns and

* *Popular Religion and Folklore of Northern India*, pp. 269, 395.

† The Malayalis say a fair boy.

‡ Mateer's *Land of Charity*, pp. 186, 187.

fireworks, in the dragging of the idol car by tumultuous noisy crowds, in singing and dancing, in the incantations and sleight of hand tricks of the priests, and in all sorts of shows, noises, and riots. On the occasions when this worship is being performed, no one ever gives the people who are assembled any exhortation for the good of their souls, nor is any means then put on operation for the promotion of virtue, and hence the so-called worship promotes immorality instead of good morals."

It is sad to think that this state of things has continued for untold generations. All this marks a very low state of civilization. Education is now spreading and more enlightened views of religion are being diffused. All lovers of their country should endeavour to promote juster ideas of religion; so that the people, instead of accepting monstrous fables and worshipping imaginary beings, may give their Father in heaven the praise due to Him for all the blessings they enjoy.

## II. MUHAMMADAN FESTIVALS.

There are six principal Muhammadan festivals observed everywhere. There are local festivals in India instituted in honour of saints. Spiritual guides are called *pirs*, and after death they are venerated as Walis or Saints.

The chief generally recognised festivals will be described:

### 1. MUHARRAM.

Muharram, the name of the first month of the Muslim year, has now become the name by which are known the days of mourning spent by the Shiahs in commemoration of the martyrdoms of Ali, and of his sons ! Hasan and Husain. The ceremonies differ in different countries.

Some days before the feast, the Ashur Khana (ten-day house) is prepared. A spot is marked where the bonfire is to be lit. Every night during the festival these fires are kindled, and the people, both old and young, fence across the fire with swords or sticks, or jump about hundreds of times calling out "Ali! Noble Husain! Bridegroom! Friend!" &c.

The Taziahs, or Tabuts, are structures made of bamboos, covered with tinsel and profusely ornamented. They are intended to represent the tomb erected on the plains of Karbala over the remains of Husain. Large sums are sometimes spent on these Taziahs. At the back of the Taziahs are laid articles similar to those supposed to have been used by Husain at Karbala,—a turban of gold, a rich sword, a shield, a bow and arrow. The usual standard is that of a hand placed on a pole. This is emblematic

10

of the five members who composed the family of the prophet and is the special standard of the Shiahs.

Every evening large crowds of people assemble in the Ashur Khanas. A band of singers chant the Marsiya, a poem in honour of Husain. At each pause the hearers beat their breasts and say "Husain! Husain!" After this the *Wáqia Khán*, (narrator of events) ascends the pulpit and gives a graphic account of the death of Husain. Sometimes he becomes very excited, and the audience is stirred up to great enthusiasm. The hearers sway their bodies to and fro, crying out, "Ali! Ali! Husain! Husain!" Each one beats his breast. This is done sometimes so vigorously as to cause blood to flow. This continues till they are well-nigh exhausted.

On the seventh day the Alam-i-Qasím is taken out in public procession. This is to represent the marriage of Qasím, the son of Hasan, to the favourite daughter of Husain, just before the death of the latter. The event is commemorated by the bearing of Qasím's standard in procession. The crowd shout out: "Bridegroom! Bridegroom!" After going through the principal streets, the standard is brought back to the Ashur Khana. As the standard which represents Qasím is supposed to be a martyr, it is then laid down, covered over, and treated as a corpse. Lamentation is made over it as for one dead.

The Neza, a spear with a lime on the top, to recall to remembrance that Husain's head was thus carried about, is taken in procession. Another standard has the representation of a horse shoe, meant to remind the people of the swift horse of Husain. Vows are frequently made to this standard. Thus a woman may say to it, "Should I, through your favour, be blessed with offspring, I shall make it run in your procession."

If two standards meet, they are made to touch as if embracing. The Buráq, supposed to represent the horse sent by Gabriel for Muhammad on the night ascent to heaven, is also taken out.

On the tenth night the whole of the Taziahs and standards are taken in procession. It is a scene of great confusion, for men and boys, disguised in all sorts of devices, run about. Respectable Muslims should seek to put it down as a disgrace to their religion.

On the following day, they kindle the fires, and say a Fátihah in each Ashur Khana. After this the standards and Taziahs are taken away to a large open spot near water, which represents the plain of Karbala. Another Fátihah is said, the ornaments are taken off the Taziahs, the frame-works of which are then cast into the water. The water reminds the people of the parching thirst which Husain felt before his death. The Taziahs during the first ten days are supposed to contain the bodies of the martyrs; but now, being empty, they can be destroyed.

Indian Musalmans have copied in their feast many Hindu ceremonies. The procession of the Taziahs and the casting them into the water, is very similar to the procession at the Durgá Puja. The oblations offered at different shrines are similar to those offered by the Hindus, such as rice, ghee, and flowers.

## 2. Akhir-i-Char Shamba.

This festival is held on the last Wednesday of the month Safar, the second of the Muhammadan year. It is observed as a feast in commemoration of Muhammad's having experienced some mitigation of his last illness and having bathed. It was the last time he performed the legal bathing, for he died on the 12th day of the next month. In some parts of Islam in the early morning of this day some verses from the Koran are written in which *salám* 'peace' occurs. They are briefly as follows: (1) Peace shall be to the word. (2) Peace be on Noah and on all creatures. (3) Peace be on Abraham. (4) Peace be on Moses and Aaron. (5) Peace be on Elias. (6) Peace be on you. (7) It is peace until the breaking of the morn. While the ink is still wet, it is washed off and the mixture drunk by the person for whom it was written, as a charm against evil.

This festival is not observed by the Wahhábis.

## 3. Bara Wafat.

This festival is held on the twelfth day of the month, Rabi u'l-Awwal, the third month of the Muhammadan year. The name is derived from bárá (Urdu) 'twelve' and *wafát*, death. It is observed in commemoration of Muhammed's death.

It seems to be a day instituted by the Muhammadans of India, and is not observed universally amongst the Muslims of all countries. On this day *Fátihahs* are recited for Muhammad's soul, and both in private houses and in mosques portions of the Traditions and other works in praise of the Prophet's excellences are read.

Some persons possess a stone with the impression of a footstep on it. On this day the place in which it is kept is decorated, and the story of the Prophet's birth, miracles, and death are repeated.

In Madras and in some other parts, instead of the stone with the impression of a footstep, a supposed portion of the Prophet's beard is exhibited. On this day it is put into rose-water, which those present then drink and rub on their eyes. Great virtue is attributed to this proceeding.

## 4. Shab Barat.

This festival is observed on the fourteenth day of the month Sha'bán, the eighth month of the Muhammadan year.

The word *Barát* means book or record. On this night Muhammad said, God registers annually all the actions of mankind which they are to perform during the coming year, and that all the children of men who are to be born and die in the year, are recorded.

On the thirteenth day food is prepared for the poor and a Fátihah for the benefit of deceased uncestors and relations is said over it. After some chapters of the Koran are read, a prayer is offered in which God is asked to transfer the reward of this service and of the charity shown in the gift of food to the poor to the souls of deceased relations and friends of this family.

The following prayer occurs in the Fátihah: "O our God, by the merits of the Apostleship of Muhammad, grant that the lamps which are lit on this holy night may be for the dead a pledge of the light eternal, which we pray thee to shed on them. O God, admit them, we beseech Thee unto the abode of eternal felicity."

The men go to the mosque, where after repetition three times of a chapter of the Koran and prayers, they rise and go to the various cemeteries. On the way they purchase flowers to place on the graves. The very pious spend the whole night in going from one cemetery to another.

These observances are works of supererogation. The rejoicing of the fourteenth day has no religious significance. The night of the fifteenth is the Guy Fawkes night of Islam. Large sums are spent on fireworks, of which more are let off at this festival than at any other.

## 5. Ramazan and 'Idu'l-Fitr.

Ramazán, the ninth month of the Muslim year, is considered peculiarly sacred, for it was in this month that Muhammad returned from meditation. The name is said to be derived from *ramz*, 'to burn.'

The observance of this month is one of the five pillars of practice in the Muslim religion. Its excellence is much extolled by Muhammad, who said that during the Ramazán "the gates of Paradise are open, and the gates of hell are shut, and the devils are chained by the leg, and only those who observe it will be permitted to enter by the gate of heaven called Rayyán." Those who keep the fast will be pardoned all their venial sins.

The fast does not commence until some Muslim is able to state that he has seen the new moon. If the sky is overclouded and the moon cannot be seen, the fast begins upon the completion of thirty days from beginning of the previous month.

It must be kept by every Muslim, except the sick, the infirm, and pregnant women, or women who are nursing their children. Young children, who have not yet reached the age of puberty, are exempted, and also travellers on a journey of more than three days. In the case of a sick person or traveller, the month's fast must be kept as soon as they are able to perform it.

Fasting is defined to be abstinence from food, drink, and cohabitation from sunrise to sunset. When the Ramazán happens to fall in the summer and the days are long, the prohibition even to drink a drop of water to slake the thirst is a very great hardship. The rich classes by turning day into night avoid much of its rigour. Those who have to work for their living find the observance of the fast very difficult, but as a rule they observe it strictly. Some Muslims when sick would not break the fast to save their lives.

During each night in Ramazán a thirtieth part of the Koran is recited in the mosque. Additional forms of prayers are repeated after the night prayer.

Devout Muslims seclude themselves for some time in the mosque during this month, and abstain from all worldly conversation, engaging themselves in the reading of the Koran.

When the thirty days have passed, the fast is broken. The first day on which food is taken is called the Idu'l-Fitr, the "Feast of the breaking of the Fast."

Mrs. Mir Hasan-Ali gives the following account of the way in which the Idu'l-Fitr is spent by Muhammadan women:

> "The assemblies of the ladies on this 'Id are marked by all the amusements and indulgences they can possibly invent and enjoy in their secluded state. Some receiving, others paying visits in covered conveyances; all doing honour to the day by wearing their best jewellery and splendid dresses. The Zenána rings with festive songs and loud music. The cheerful meeting of friends, the distribution of presents to dependents and remembrances to the poor; all is life and joy, cheerful bustle and amusement on this happy day of 'Id when the good lady of the mansion sits in state to receive presents from inferiors and to grant proofs of her favour to others."*

## 6. Baqar 'Id.

This is the most important festival of the whole year. It is also known as the Idúz-Zuhá, the 'feast of sacrifice,' and Idu'l-Azha.

In Turkey it is called *Bairám*, "The Cow Festival." The idolatrous Arabs had been in the habit of offering animals in sacrifice as a part of the concluding ceremony of the pilgrimage

* *Observations on the Musalmans of India*, p. 192.

to Mecca. At the time when the Arabs were sacrificing victims at Mecca, Muhammad went forth from his house at Medina, and assembling his followers instituted the Baqar 'Id. Two young kids were brought before him. One he sacrificed and said: "O Lord! I sacrifice this for my whole people, all those who bear witness to thy unity and to my mission. O Lord! this is for Muhammad, and for the whole family of Muhammad."

Great merit is obtained by all who keep this feast. Ayesha relates how the Prophet once said: "Man hath not done anything on the 'Idu'l-Azha more pleasing to God than spilling blood; for verily the animal sacrificed will come on the day of resurrection with its horns, hair and hoofs, and will make the scale of his good actions very heavy. Verily its blood reached the acceptance of God before it falleth upon the ground, therefore be joyful in it."

If the victim is a camel, it must be placed with the head towards Mecca. Its front legs being bandaged together, the sacrificer must stand on the right hand side of the victim, and plunge the knife into its throat with such force that the animal may fall at once. Any other mode of slaying it is unlawful. The operator says: "O God, from Thee and to Thee (I do this), in the name of God, God is Great!"

It is considered highly meritorious to sacrifice one animal for each member of the family; but as this would involve an expenditure which few could bear, it is allowable to sacrifice one victim for the household.

The advantages of observing this feast are thus set forth in a sermon:

"Know, O servants of God! that to rejoice on the feast day is the sign and mark of the pure and good. Exalted will be the rank of such in Paradise, especially on the day of resurrection will they obtain dignity and honour.

"If you sacrifice a fat animal it will serve you well, and carry you across the Sirát (the bridge across hell). O Believers, thus said the Prophet, on whom be the mercy and peace of God. 'Sacrifice the victim with your own hands;' this was the Sunnat of Ibrahim, on whom be peace."

One explanation of the feast is that it is in memory of Abraham attempting to sacrifice Ishmael, but that Gabriel substituted a sheep for the lad.

The Baqar-'Id and the 'Idú'l-Fitr constitute the two great feasts of Islam. A country in which Musalmans could not observe them both would at once become Dáru'l-Harb, or House of Enmity, in which it would be the duty of every Muslim to join in a Jihád against the rulers of the land.

## Festivals in honour of Pirs.

Among other practices borrowed from the Hindus must be placed the pilgrimage made by Indian Musalmans to the shrines of Pirs or Saints, the ceremonies connected with them, and the festivals instituted in their honour.

The title of Pír given to a Musalman devotee is equivalent to the term Guru amongst the Hindus. A man who seeks to be a 'religious' takes a Pír as a spiritual guide. "Follow," says the poet Walí, "the footsteps of thy Pír like a shadow." After death these Pírs are venerated as Walís or Saints. The Pírs, when alive, are frequently resorted to form a ta'wíz or charm, and the aid of their prayers is often invoked. The sepulchre of a Walí is called a Dargáh, shrine; Mazár, place of pilgrimage; Rauzah, garden. The professional reciter of the Koran at such places is called Rauzah Khán. As a rule processions are made to the shrines, and flowers, sweetmeats, and food, over which a Fátihah, has been said are offered. Usually the Fátihah is *for* the Saint, not *to* the Saint. It is considered a very meritorious act to give land for the erection of such shrines, and to endow them.*

An account of one of the principal festivals of this kind will be given as a specimen:

## Festival of Qadir Wali Sahib.

This is the great Saint of Southern India. The 'Urs† is celebrated on the tenth day of the sixth month of the Muhammadan year. The shrine is at Nagore, a town situated four miles north of Negapatam. He is the patron saint of sailors, who in times of difficulty vow that, if they reach the shore in safety, they will offer a Fátihah in the name of Qádir Walí. The common people have a profound faith in the power of the saint to work miracles.

This festival affords a curious illustration of the way in which Hindu influences have acted upon Islám, and how even Hindus pay regard to Muslim Saints. After the death of Qádir Walí a small mosque was erected on or near his tomb. The fame of the Walí gradually grew, and a Hindu Raja made a vow that if he was blessed with the birth of a son, he would enlarge and beautify the mosque. His wish was fulfilled, and the present elegant structure is the result. So famous has the shrine of the Saint now become that the Musalmans say: "First Mecca, then Nagore." The same reason which induced the Hindu Raja to make a votive

---

* Sell's *Faith of Islam*, pp. 326, 327.

† The Ceremonies at the anniversary of a Saint, called 'Ooroos' in the Madras Almanack.

offering years ago still influences large numbers of people. On Thursday evenings, the commencement of the Muhammadan Sabbath, many Hindu women resort to the shrine of the Saint.

## General Remarks.

There are many other Walis and Pirs to whose tombs pilgrimages are made and in memory of whom many superstitious observances are still kept up; but all such pilgrimages to a Dargáh (shrine) are no necessary part of Islám. In all parts of the country there are the shrines of Saints who have a local reputation, and where annual festivals are more or less observed.*

* Abridged from Sell's *Faith of Islam*, pp. 330—332.